S. M. Brown

Missionary Triumph

being a collection of songs suitable for all kinds of missionary services

S. M. Brown

Missionary Triumph

being a collection of songs suitable for all kinds of missionary services

ISBN/EAN: 9783337265700

Printed in Europe, USA, Canada, Australia, Japan

Cover: Foto ©Lupo / pixelio.de

More available books at **www.hansebooks.com**

Missionary ✳ Triumph:

BEING A COLLECTION OF

Songs Suitable for all kinds of
Missionary Services.

— BY —

S. M. BROWN and J. M. HUNT.

CINCINNATI:
Published by The JOHN CHURCH CO., 74 W. Fourth St.

CHICAGO:
ROOT & SONS MUSIC CO.
200 WABASH AVENUE.

NEW YORK:
THE J. CHURCH CO.,
19 EAST 16TH ST.

PREFACE.

In all the range of song books published in this country, there is not one on the great and absorbing subject of MISSIONS. We therefore offer the following pages without apology, praying for the speedy TRIUMPH of the cause of Jesus among all kindred and tongues.

We hereby express our thanks to the many authors who have so liberally contributed to these pages.

S. M. BROWN.
J. M. HUNT.

No. 2.   Little Gleaner's Band.

"*Go work to-day in my vineyard.*"—MATT. 21:28.

LAURA C. NURSE.   FRANK M. DAVIS, by per.

1. See the fields are white for har-vest, And the reap-ers are so few;
2. Lit-tle hands must be the gar-ner For the pre-cious seeds of truth;
3. Lit-tle words so soft-ly spo-ken, Bring the wayward souls to God;
4. Lit-tle songs shall swell the chorus In the ransomed choirs a-bove;

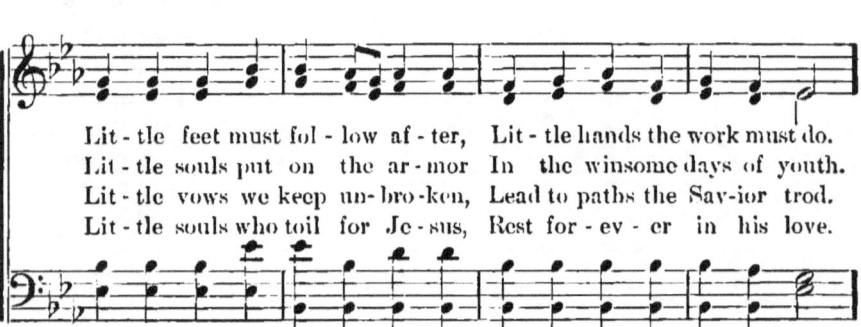

Lit-tle feet must fol-low af-ter, Lit-tle hands the work must do.
Lit-tle souls put on the ar-mor In the winsome days of youth.
Lit-tle vows we keep un-bro-ken, Lead to paths the Sav-ior trod.
Lit-tle souls who toil for Je-sus, Rest for-ev-er in his love.

CHORUS.

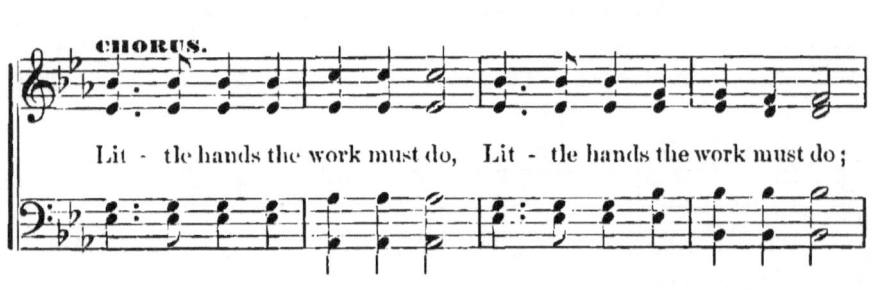

Lit-tle hands the work must do, Lit-tle hands the work must do;

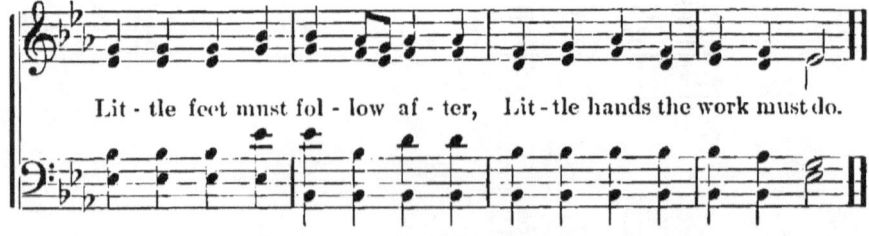

Lit-tle feet must fol-low af-ter, Lit-tle hands the work must do.

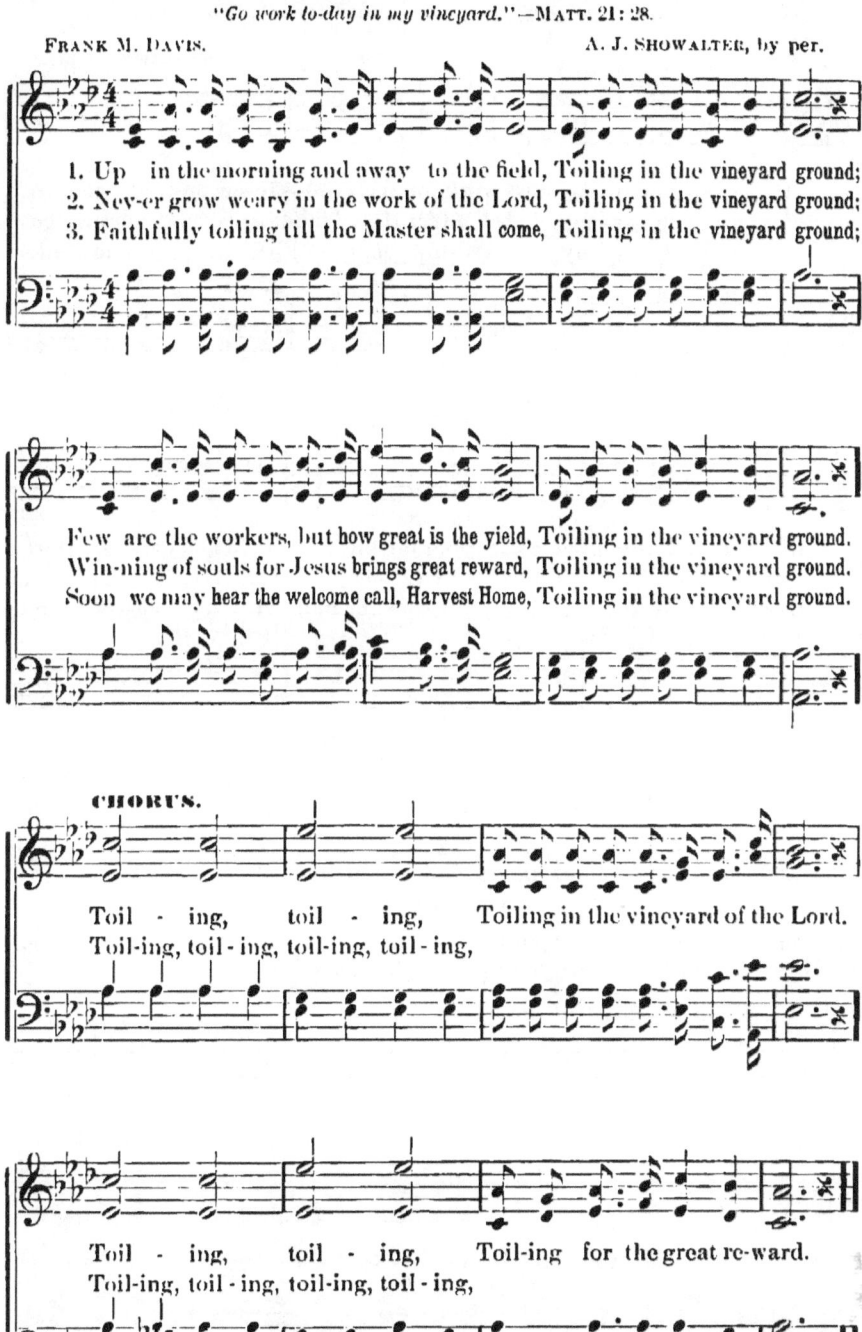

No. 4. Come, Join the Army.

"Come thou faithful unto death, and I will give thee a crown of life."—REV. 2: 10.

J. M. HUNT. S. M. BROWN, by per.

March time.

1. Come join the ar-my, and work for the Lord—Jesus entreats you in
2. Come join the ar-my, and stand for the right; Strong is our Captain—go
3. Come join the ar-my, its hardships endure: Firm like a sol-dier, 'midst

his bless-ed word: Come with your buckler, your shield and your sword; Come
forth in his might; Un-furl the ban-ner a-gainst Satan's blight, With
Sa-tan's al-lure; Stand by your col-ors and vic-t'ry se-cure—Send

CHORUS.

share a soldier's conflicts and a saint's reward.
true and loy-al courage put the foe to flight. Come and join the army, the
down the line the watchword, "Our reward is sure."

tried and the true; Come and join the army, there's work for you; Come and join the

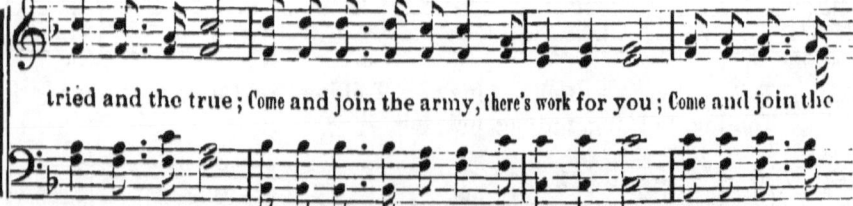

Copyright, 1888, by BROWN & HUNT.

Come, Join the Army. Concluded.

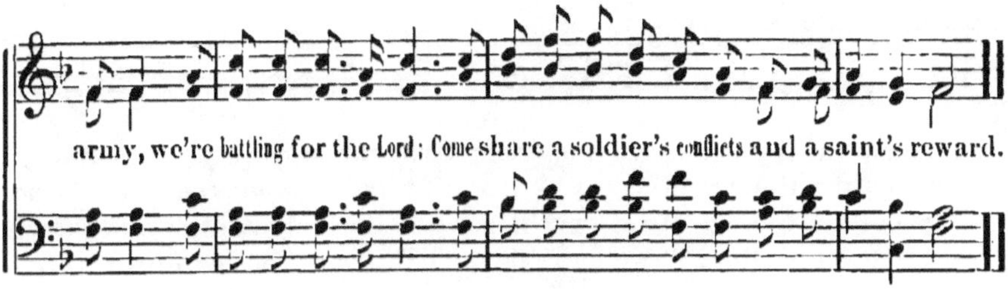

army, we're battling for the Lord; Come share a soldier's conflicts and a saint's reward.

No. 5.   Trust On.
J. M. HUNT.

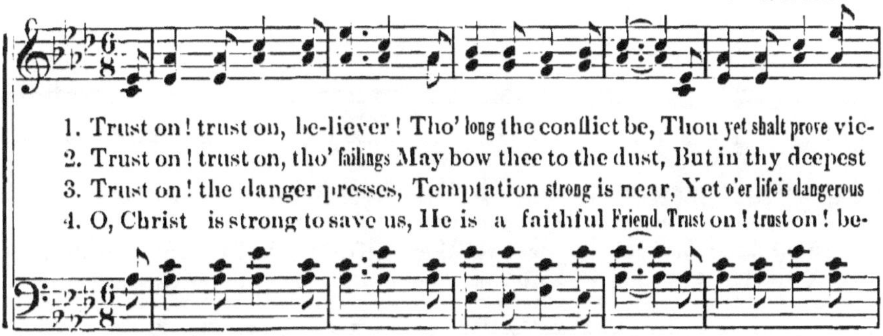

1. Trust on! trust on, be-liever! Tho' long the conflict be, Thou yet shalt prove vic-
2. Trust on! trust on, tho' failings May bow thee to the dust, But in thy deepest
3. Trust on! the danger presses, Temptation strong is near, Yet o'er life's dangerous
4. O, Christ is strong to save us, He is a faithful Friend. Trust on! trust on! be-

torious; Thy God shall fight for thee.
sorrow, O give not up thy trust.
rap-ids, He will thy pass-age steer.
liev-er, O trust him to the end.

CHORUS.
Trust on! trust on! Trust on! trust on! Tho' dark the night and drear, Trust on, trust on! The morn-ing dawn is near.

7

No. 6. Shout the Tidings.

S. M. Brown. J. M. Hunt, by per.

1. Shout the ti-dings of sal-va-tion, Send the gospel's joy-ous sound,
2. Shout the ti-dings of sal-va-tion, To the thousands near your home,
3. Shout the ti-dings of sal-va-tion,—See the nations press your shore—
4. Shout the ti-dings of sal-va-tion, Till the nations own their King;

Till the precious in-vi-ta-tion, Spread to earth's re-mot-est bound.
Till your own be-lov-ed na-tion, To the feet of Je-sus come.
Sound the gos-pel in-vi-ta-tion, To the heathen at your door.
Till in joy-ous ex-ul-ta-tion, Ev-'ry vale and mount shall sing.

CHORUS.

Send the news, the glad, good news. From the rising to the setting of the sun,

Till the nations come and be-fore the throne, The great Redeemer own.

No. 7. Rally to the Master's Call.

"Go work to-day in my vineyard."—MATT. 21: 28.

FRANK M. DAVIS.   T. C. O'KANE, by per.

1. In the vineyard of the Lord go work to-day, Ral-ly to the Master's call;
2. To the vineyard then away, ere morning sun Ris-es in the heavens high;
3. Youthful workers, then, go forth to work for God In the fields already white;

While the laborers are few, the fields are white; Hasten, there is work for all.
Give the early hours to God, for great reward Shall be giv-en by and by.
He is calling you to work while yet 'tis day, Hasten ere the coming night.

REFRAIN.

Work for all, work for all, In the vineyard of the Lord there is
Work for all, work for all,

work for all; Work for all, work for all, Rally to the Master's call.
Work for all, work for all,

No. 8. The Widow's Mite.

MARK 12: 42.

S. M. BROWN. S. M. BROWN, by per.

1. O - ver a - gainst the treas'ry of the Lord, See the Mas-ter
2. One there is among them, un-no-ticed by the throng, As in pomp and
3. But a sin - gle farthing is all she has to give, Yet the Mas-ter

sit - ting, a - mid the surging crowd; Lo! the throng is com-ing, to
splendor the great ones pass a - long; But the heart of Je - sus is
knows it is her on-ly means to live; Hear the words of Je - sus, as

bring their treasures rare; From a-bund-ant rich-es they their love declare.
kin-dled to a flame, As she makes her off'ring for the hon-or of his name.
from his lips they fall: "Out of her deep poverty she's given more than all."

CHORUS.

Sitting there in silence, he's watching yet to - day, Weighing what they

3 King of glory, reign forever,
  Thine, an everlasting crown;
Nothing from thy love shall sever
  Those whom thou hast made thine own;
    Happy objects of thy grace,
    Chosen to behold thy face.

4 Savior, hasten thine appearing;
  Bring, O, bring the glorious day,
When the awful summons hearing,
  Heaven and earth shall pass away;
    Then with golden harps we'll sing,
    "Glory, glory to our King!"

No. 10.   **In the Cross.**

"*God forbid that I should glory, save in the cross of our Lord Jesus Christ.*"—GAL. 6: 11.

JOHN BOWRING.   CHAS. EDW. POLLOCK.

1. In the cross of Christ I glo - ry, Tow'ring o'er the wrecks of time;
2. When the woes of life o'er-take me, Hopes deceive and fears an - noy,
3. When the sun of bliss is beaming Light and love up - on my way,
4. Bane and blessing, pain and pleasure, By the cross are sanc - ti - fied;

All the light of sa - cred sto - ry, Gathers 'round its head sublime.
Nev - er shall the cross for-sake me; Lo! it glows with peace and joy.
From the cross the radiance streaming, Adds new lus - tre to the day.
Peace is there that knows no measure, Joys that thro' all time a - bide.

CHORUS.

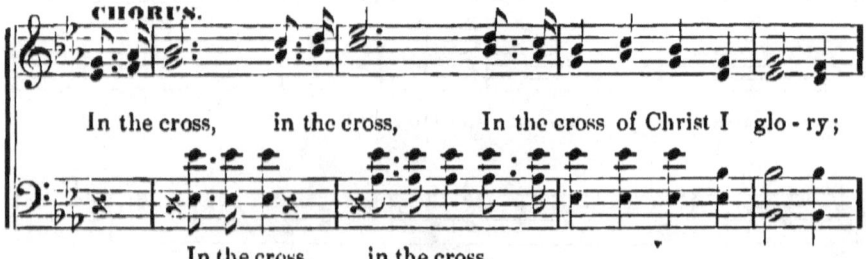

In the cross,   in the cross,   In the cross of Christ I glo - ry;
In the cross,   in the cross,

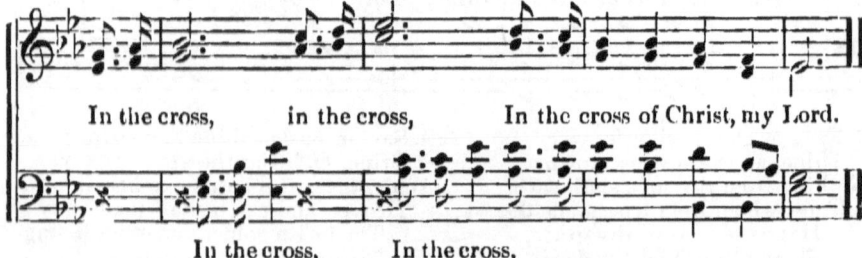

In the cross,   in the cross,   In the cross of Christ, my Lord.
In the cross,   In the cross,

No. 11. Cling to the Bible.

M. J. Smith.
J. R. Murray, by per.

1. Cling to the Bi-ble, tho' all else be tak-en; Lose not its prom-is-es precious and sure; Souls that are sleep-ing its ech-oes a-wak-en,
2. Cling to the Bi-ble, this jew-el, this treasure Brings to us hon-or and saves fall-en man; Pearl whose great value no mor-tal can measure,
3. Lamp for the feet that in byways have wandered, Guide for the youth that would oth-er-wise fall; Hope for the sin-ner whose best days are squand-ered,

Drink from the foun-tain, so peaceful, so pure.
Seek and se-cure it, O soul, while you can. Cling to the Bi-ble!
Staff for the a-ged, and best book of all.

CHORUS.

Cling to the Bi-ble! Cling to the Bi-ble, Our Lamp and our Guide.

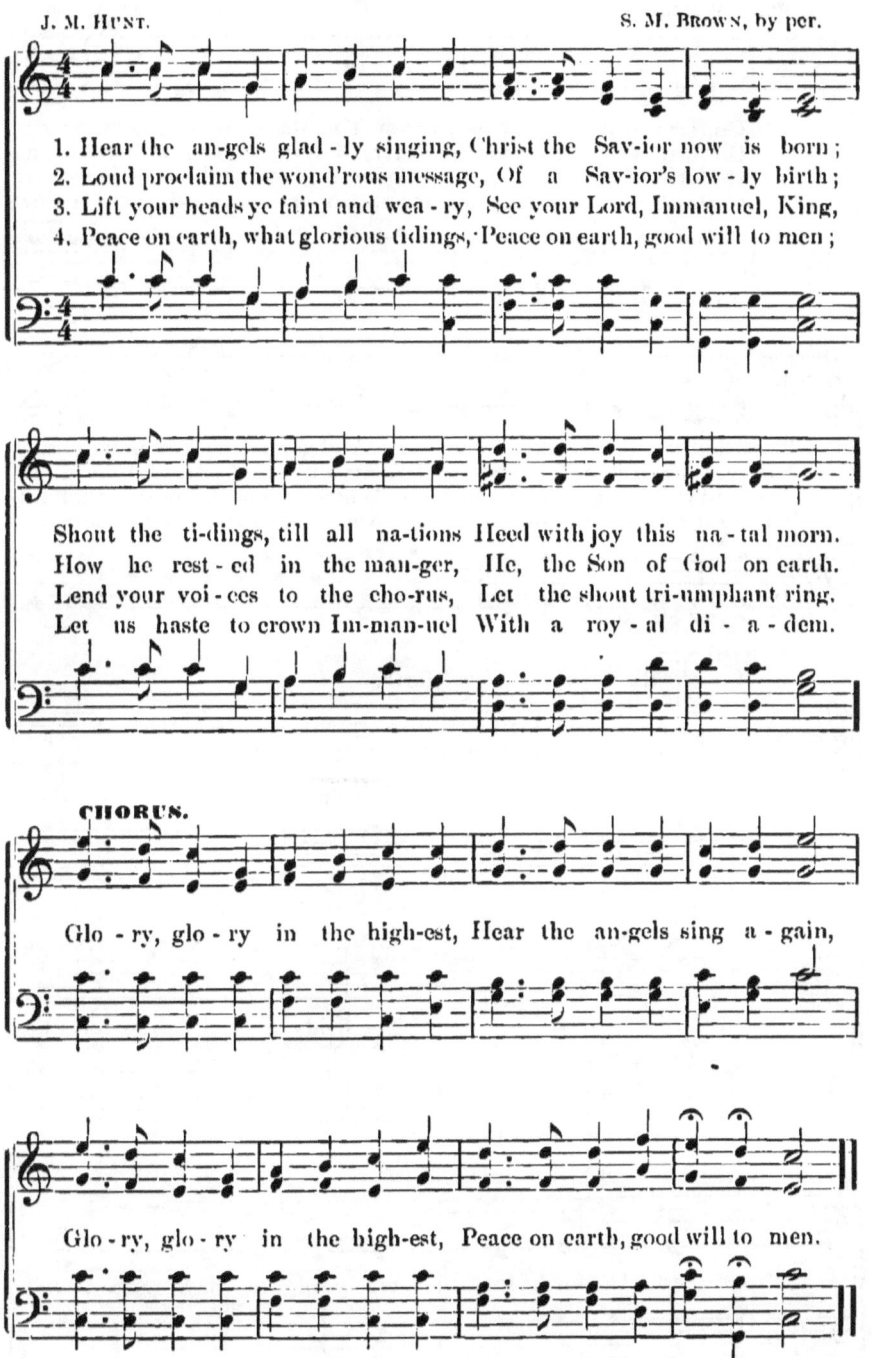

No. 15. Cometh A Blessing Down.

Mary Francis Tyler.   S. M. Brown.

1. Not to a man of dol - lars, Not to a man of deeds,
2. Not un - to lands ex - pan - sion, Not to a mis - er's chest,
3. Not to the fol - ly blind - ed, Not to the steeped in shame,
4. But un - to one whose spir - it Yearns for the great and good;

Not un - to craft or cun - ning, Not un - to hu-man creeds,
Not to the prince-ly man - sion, Not to a blossomed crest,
Not to the car - nal mind - ed, Not to un - ho - ly fame,
Un - to the one whose store-house Yield-eth the hungry food;

Not to the one whose pas - sion Is for a world's re-nown,
Not to the sor - did world - ling, Not to the knav-ish clown,
Not in neglect of du - ty, Not in the jew-eled crown,
Un - to the one who la - bors Fear-less of foe or frown,

Not in a form of fash - ion Com - eth a blessing down.
Not to the haughty ty - rant Com - eth a blessing down.
Not at the smile of beau - ty Com - eth a blessing down.
Un - to the kind-ly - heart - ed Com - eth a blessing down.

Oh, Where are the Reapers. Concluded.

who will help us to gar-ner in The sheaves of good from the fields of sin.

No. 17. Who will Reply?

"*White already to harvest.*"—JOHN 4: 35.

P. P. BLISS.   JAS. McGRANAHAN, by per.

1. The fields are white, 'tis har-vest time, The la - bor-ors are few;
2. Faint heart, no long - er i - dly stand, Nor yet an hour de - lay;

The Lord un - to his serv-ice calls The will - ing and the true.
The gath'ring clouds a storm foretell; A-rise, go, work to - day.

CHORUS.

Hear ye the call, . . . who will re - ply? . . . Send me, O
earn-est call, oh, who'll re-ply?

Master, here am I.
here am I.

3 Wait not for other hands to do
    The service of the Lord;
 "To every man his work" is given,
    And each receives reward.

4 What wondrous grace, O Lord, is thine,
    Such servants to employ,
 To make us partners in thy toil,
    And sharers in thy joy!
CHO.–I hear the call, I now reply,
    Send me, O Master, here am I.

No. 18.   Look unto the Fields.

JOHN 4: 35.

T. P. W.   THOS. P. WESTENDORF, by per.

1. Go ye out to the fields for the harvest is ready, Go help the Master
2. The dew and the sunlight have fallen from heaven, God in his mercy
3. Angels watch from above while the daylight is dying, Loudly they call, for

gath-er the grain; Arouse from thy slumber, the day is de-clin-ing,
giv-eth the rain; Sweet breath of the morn and the shadows of e - ven,
reapers are few; With sickle in hand and with feet swiftly fly - ing,

CHORUS.

Night com-eth soon, when hope will be vain.
All, all have helped to rip - en the grain. Look un-to the fields, yes,
Has - ten, my broth-er, God needeth you.

Look un - to the fields, For they are white, all read - y to har-vest;

Look unto the fields, yes, Look unto the fields, for they are ready to harvest.

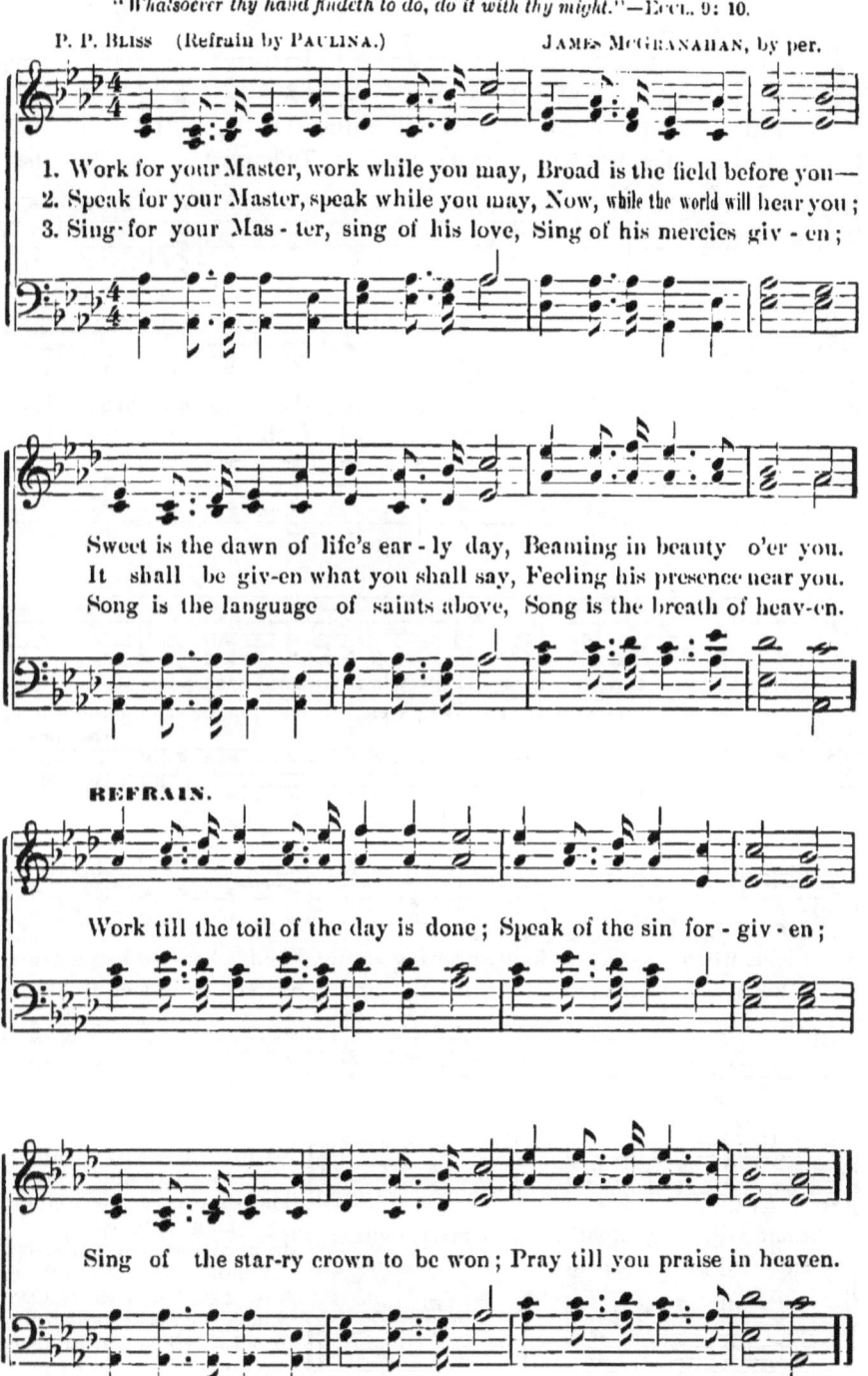

No. 20. Now is the Harvest Time.

Rev. J. O. Foster, A. M.
G. F. Root, by per.

March movement.

1. Lift up your eyes on the fields all white, Wav-ing so full in the gos-pel light, Gold-en the grain in the sun-shine bright, The great har-vest time has come. Fields where the seed has been scattered long, Fields where the tall stalks are growing strong, Fields where the reapers now come with song, Shouting the harvest home.

2. Hear how the Mas-ter is call-ing you, Th' harvest is great, but the la-b'rors few, Reap-ers are want-ed, faith-ful ones, true, For now is the har-vest time. Wag-es of life for the strong and brave, Wheat for the gar-ner of life to save, Res-cu-ing men from a sin-ful grave, Na-tions of ev-'ry clime.

3 Others have sown where you may now reap,
Tho' they have gone to their long, long sleep,
Jesus his promises all will keep,
Behold now the harvest time.
Now is the joy of the fallen race,
Now is the fulness of gospel grace,
Now does the Master reveal his face,
Now is the harvest time.

No. 22. The Little Missionary.

J. R. M.
J. R. MURRAY, by per.

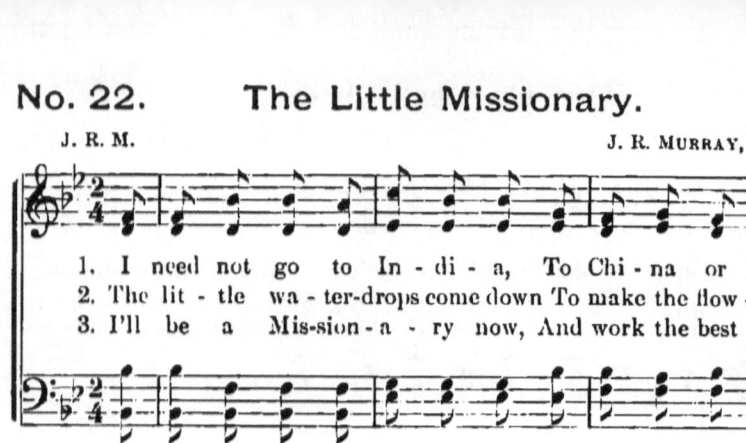

1. I need not go to In - di - a, To Chi - na or Ja - pan;
2. The lit - tle wa - ter-drops come down To make the flow - ers grow;
3. I'll be a Mis-sion - a - ry now, And work the best I may,

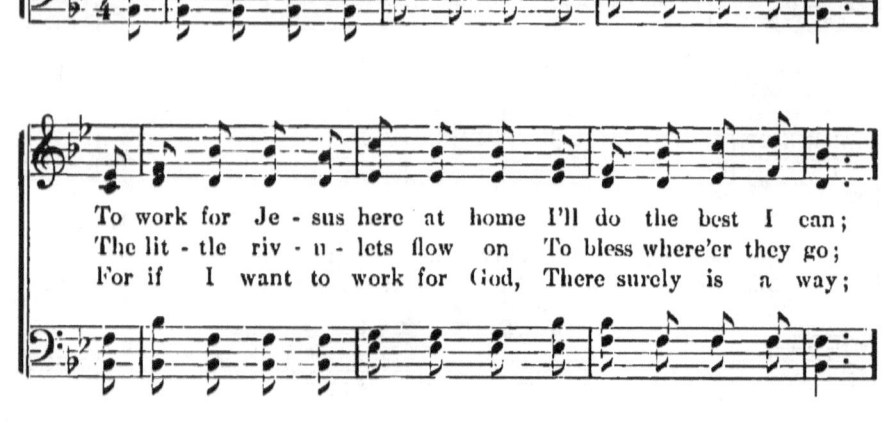

To work for Je - sus here at home I'll do the best I can;
The lit - tle riv - u - lets flow on To bless where'er they go;
For if I want to work for God, There surely is a way;

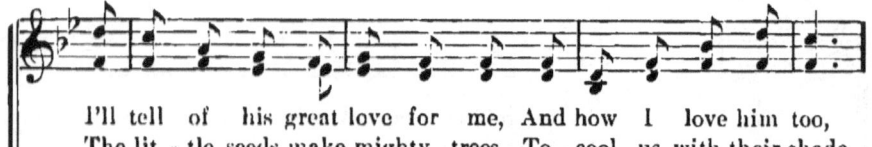

I'll tell of his great love for me, And how I love him too,
The lit - tle seeds make mighty trees, To cool us with their shade,
I'll pray for those who cross the sea, My offering, too, I'll send,

And bet - ter far, I'll show my love In all that I may do.
If lit - tle things like these do good, To try, I'm not a - fraid.
And do all that is in my power, This great bad world to mend.

The Little Missionary. Concluded.

CHORUS.

We all may work for Je-sus, Wher-ev-er we may be,
I'll try to work for Je-sus, Who did so much for me.

No. 23. What Shall we Give to God?

"Who gave himself for our sins."—GAL. 1: 4.

C. WORDSWORTH, D. D.   M. BROWN.

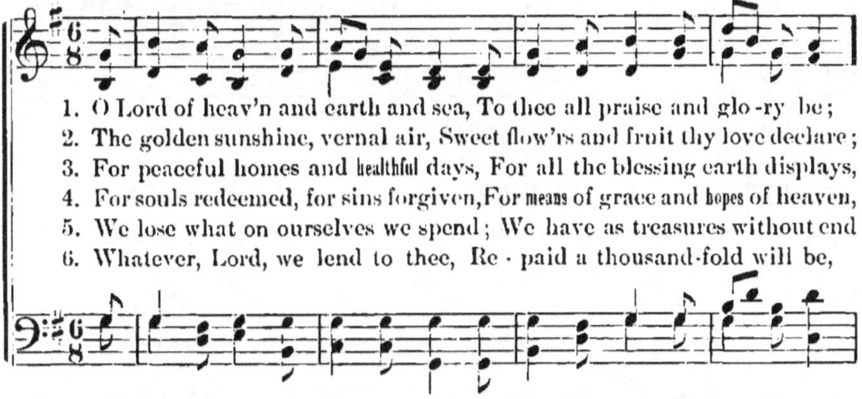

1. O Lord of heav'n and earth and sea, To thee all praise and glo-ry be;
2. The golden sunshine, vernal air, Sweet flow'rs and fruit thy love declare;
3. For peaceful homes and healthful days, For all the blessing earth displays,
4. For souls redeemed, for sins forgiven, For means of grace and hopes of heaven,
5. We lose what on ourselves we spend; We have as treasures without end
6. Whatever, Lord, we lend to thee, Re-paid a thousand-fold will be,

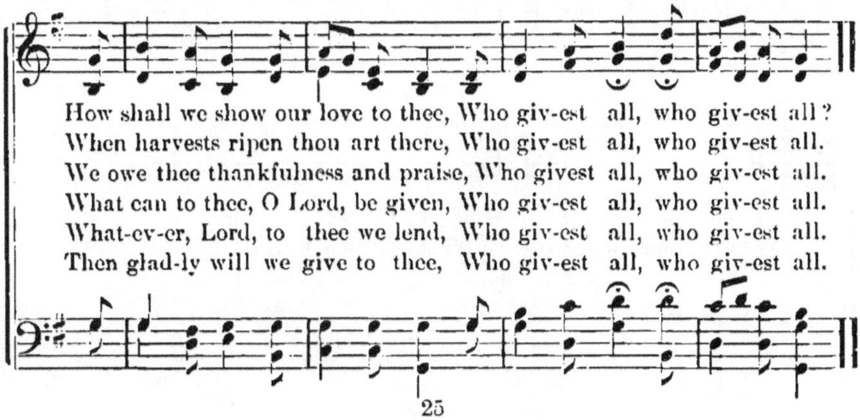

How shall we show our love to thee, Who giv-est all, who giv-est all?
When harvests ripen thou art there, Who giv-est all, who giv-est all.
We owe thee thankfulness and praise, Who givest all, who giv-est all.
What can to thee, O Lord, be given, Who giv-est all, who giv-est all.
What-ev-er, Lord, to thee we lend, Who giv-est all, who giv-est all.
Then glad-ly will we give to thee, Who giv-est all, who giv-est all.

No. 24. Open the Door.

"Suffer little children to come unto me." —LUKE 18: 16.

J. M. HUNT, by per.

1. O-pen the door for the children, Ten-der-ly gath-er them in;
2. O-pen the door for the children, See, they are coming in throngs,
3. O-pen the door for the children, Take the dear lambs by the hand,

In from the highways and hedges, In from the plac-es of sin;
Bid them sit down at the banquet, Teach them your beautiful songs,
Point them to truth and to Je-sus, Point them to heaven's bright land.

Some are so young and so help-less, Some are so hun-gry and cold;
Pray you the fa-ther to bless them, Pray you that grace may be given;
Some are so young and so help-less, Some are so hun-gry and cold;

O-pen the door for the children, Gath-er them in-to the fold.
O-pen the door for the children, Of such is the kingdom of heaven.
O-pen the door for the children, Gath-er them in-to the fold.

Open the Door. Concluded.

No. 25. The Lord's Prayer.

J. M. HUNT.

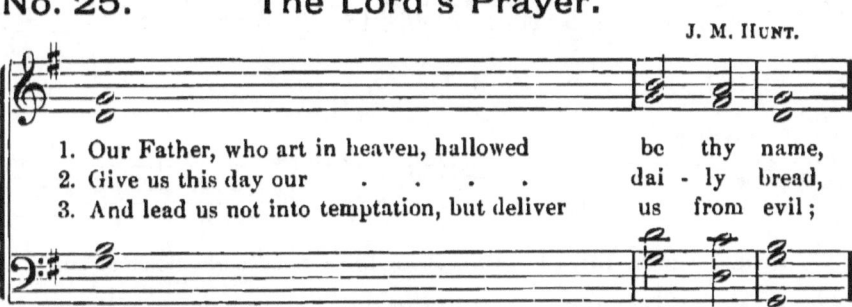

1. Our Father, who art in heaven, hallowed be thy name,
2. Give us this day our . . . . dai - ly bread,
3. And lead us not into temptation, but deliver us from evil;

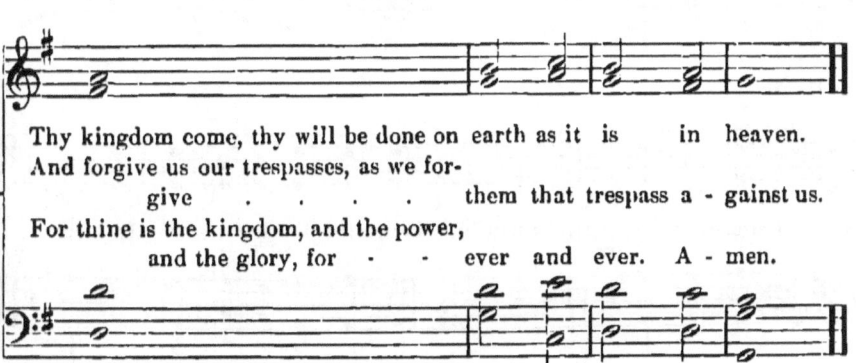

Thy kingdom come, thy will be done on earth as it is in heaven.
And forgive us our trespasses, as we for-
give . . . . them that trespass a - gainst us.
For thine is the kingdom, and the power,
and the glory, for - - ever and ever. A - men.

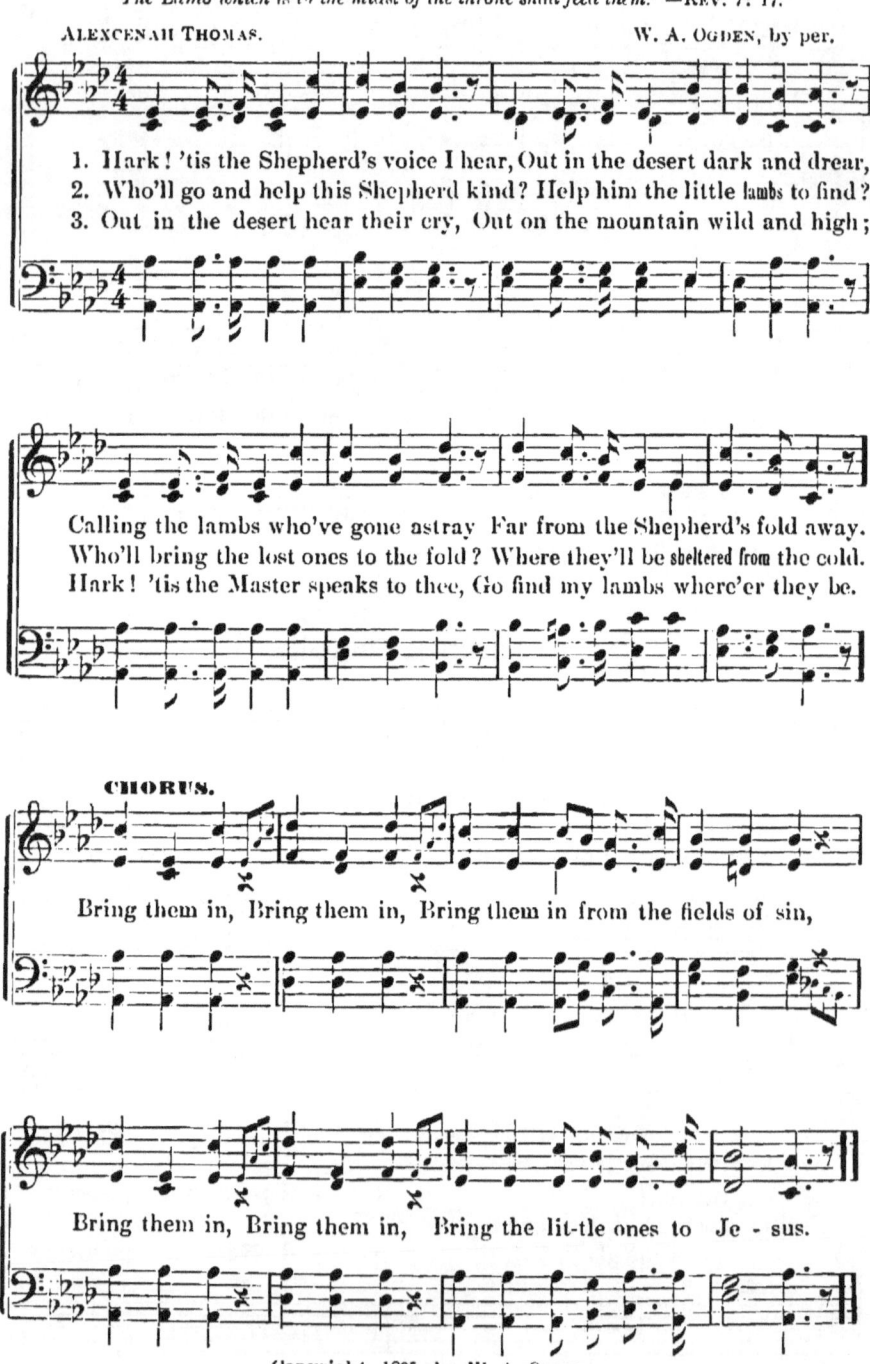

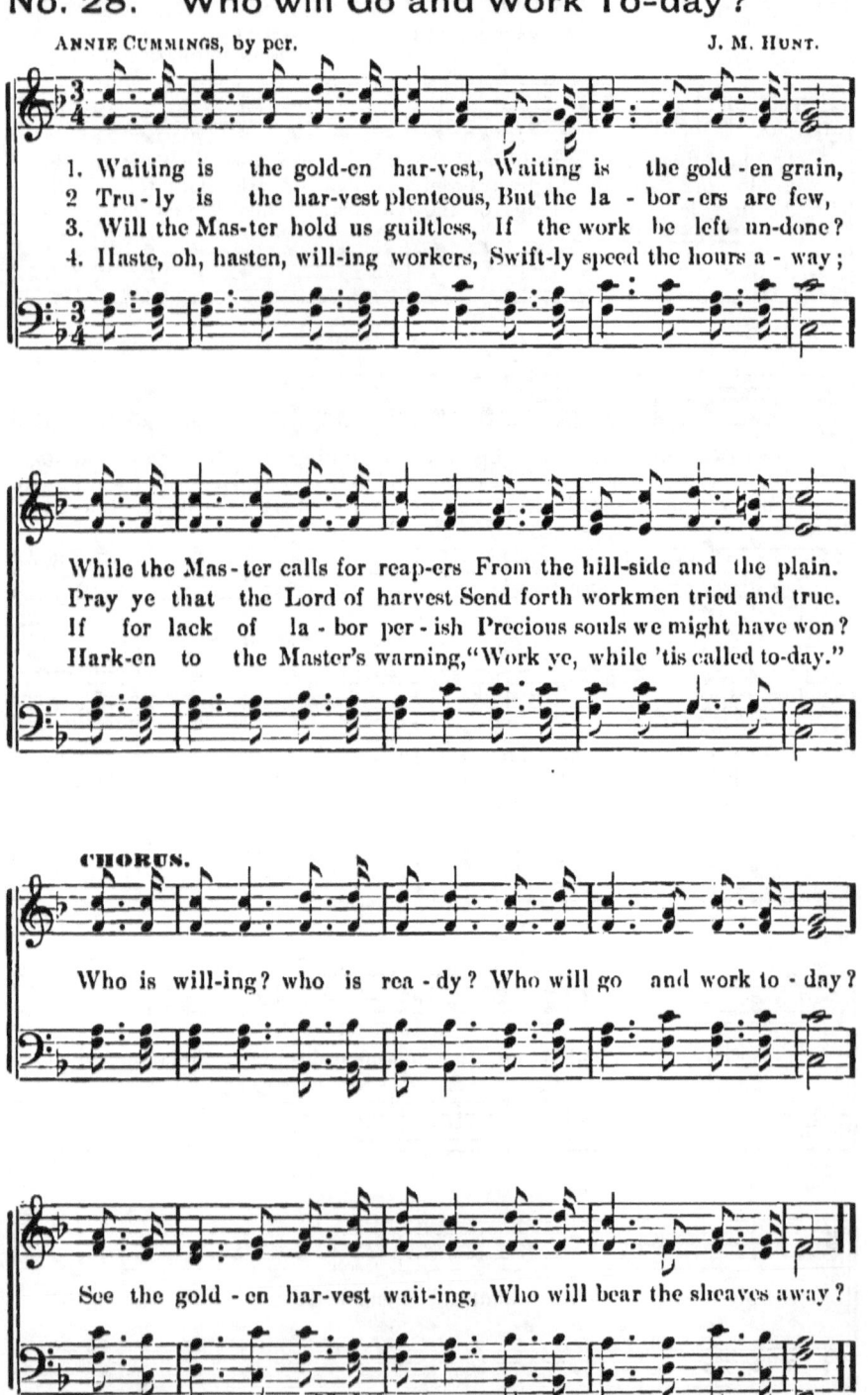

No. 30. We Will Go.

G. W. L.   G. W. LYON, by per.

1. We will go in the strength of the Master, In the path he hath made for our feet; We will fol-low the light of his coun-sel, Nor shrink from the danger we meet.
2. We will walk in the strength of the Master, In the la-bor he gives us to do; And his smile shall af-ford joy and com-fort, Our souls shall their vig-or re-new.
3. We will trust in the strength of the Master, We will trust his Omnip-o-tent arm, And his pow-er shall prove all suf-fi-cient, To shield us from danger and harm.

CHORUS.

We will go, we will go, As the Master commands we will go, And his pre-sence our steps shall at-tend, He will guard, He will guard, He will guide, He will guide, And sup-port till our journey shall end.

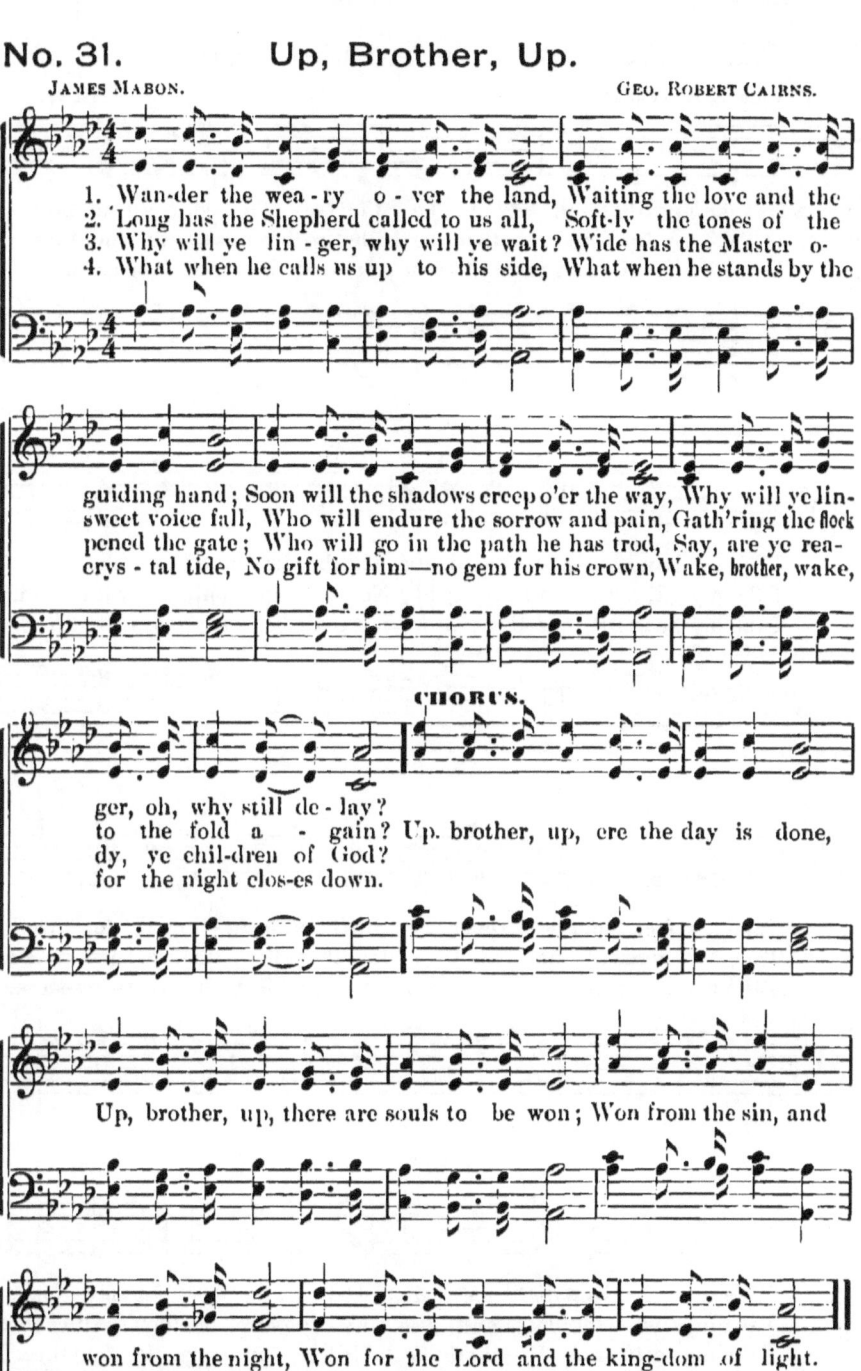

No. 33. Seeking the Lost Sheep.

J. M. Hunt, by per.

Little Gleaners. Concluded.

But we can fol-low him who reaps, And gath-er what he leaves.

No. 35. Go, Wield the Sickle's Blade.

"The harvest truly is great, but the laborers are few."—LUKE 10: 2.

S. M. BROWN.

1. Do not say, O Christian reap-er, The earth no har-vest yields;
2. Dreary au-tumn days are com-ing, The sum-mer will be o'er;

Look a-broad, and you'll dis-cov-er The wait-ing har-vest fields.
And a-mong the rip-ened har-vest You'll find your work no more.

Go ye forth with hope and courage, Go, wield the sick-le's blade,
La-bor on in faith, and gath-er The sheaves of gold-en grain;

Fear ye none of Sa-tan's reapers, Tho' well they be ar-rayed.
Then with joy you'll greet the Master, When he shall come a-gain.

Go in the Strength of Jesus. Concluded.

Toil on in faith, be-liev-ing, He will thy la-bors crown.

No. 37. The Harvest is White.
W. E. PENN. JOHN 4: 35. CHAS. EDW. POLLOCK.

1. Lift up your eyes, behold and see, The fields are white as white can be;
2. For want of men to preach the truth, In every land, to age and youth,
3. For want of men and women, too, To do whate'er they find to do,
4. For want of men both young and old, Who love their Savior more than gold,

And much we're losing ev-'ry day, For want of men to work and pray.
For Je-sus' sake to give up all, And humbly at his feet to fall.
For-sake the fol-lies of the day, And toil and labor, watch and pray.
For want of lib-'ral heart-ed men, The gospel through the earth to send.

CHORUS.

The harvest fields, O brother, see, Are just as white as white can be,

And much we're losing ev-'ry day, For want of men to work and pray.

Copyrighted by W. E. PENN. From "Harvest Bells, No. 2," by per.

No. 38. Stand up for Jesus.

CHAS. EDW. POLLOCK.

Boldly.

1. Stand up, stand up for Je - sus! Ye sol-diers of the cross;
2. Stand up, stand up for Je - sus! Stand in his strength alone;
3. Stand up, stand up for Je - sus! The strife will not be long;

Lift high his roy - al ban - ner, It must not suf - fer loss.
The arm of flesh will fail you, Ye dare not trust your own.
This day the noise of bat - tle, The next the vic - tor's song.

From vic-t'ry un - to vic - t'ry His ar - my shall be led,
Put on the gos - pel ar - mor, And watchful un - to prayer,
To him that o - ver-com - eth A crown of life shall be,

Till ev - 'ry foe is vanquished, And Christ is Lord in - deed.
Where du - ty calls or dan - ger, Be nev - er want-ing there.
He with the King of glo - ry Shall reign e - ter - nal - ly.

Stand up for Jesus. Concluded.

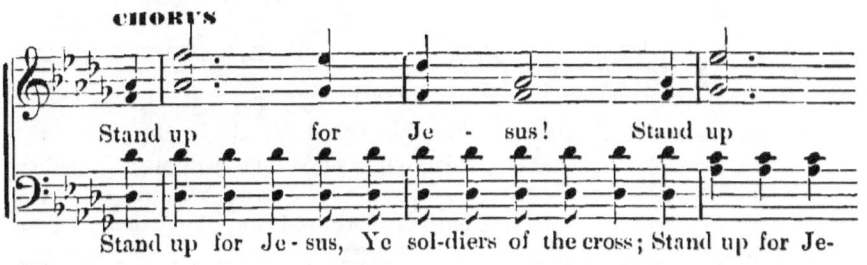

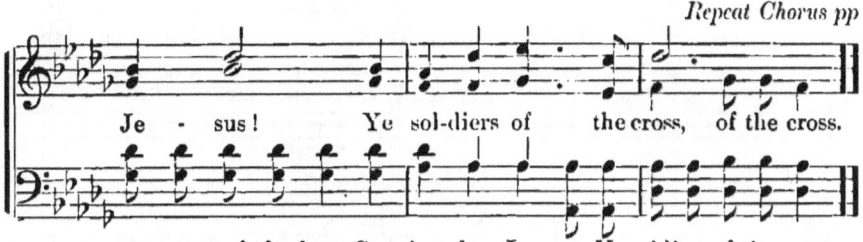

No. 39. Old Hundred. L. M.

Thos. Ken. 1697.   G. Franc. 1545.

Praise God, from whom all blessings flow; Praise him, all creatures here below; Praise him above, ye heavenly host; Praise Father, Son and Holy Ghost.

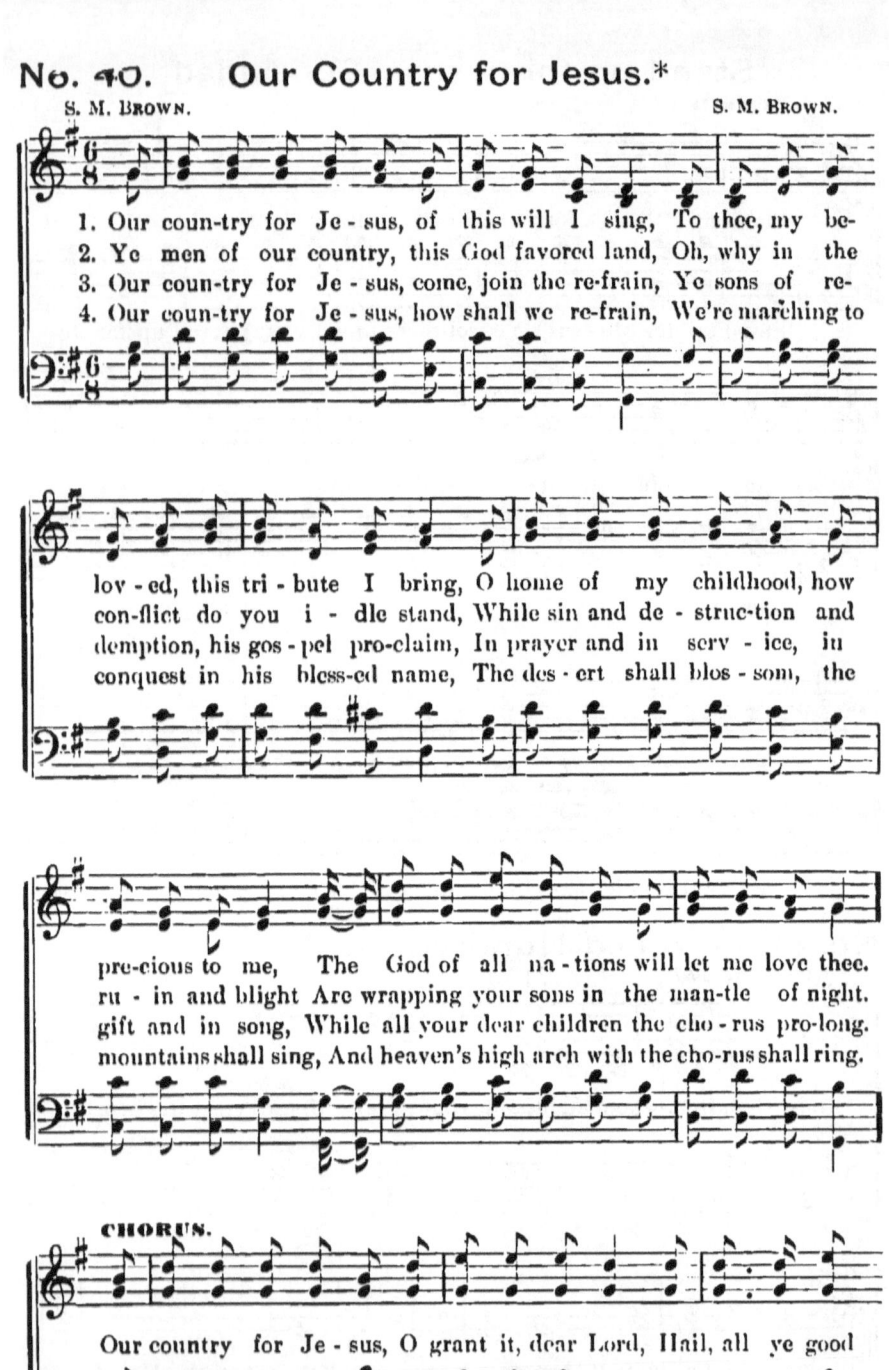

Our Country for Jesus. Concluded.

peo - ple, be this your re - ward, And when the dear Mas - ter shall bid us all come, May you and your children be safe gathered home.

No. 41. America.

S. F. Smith.

1. My country, 'tis of thee, Sweet land of lib - er - ty, Of thee I sing;
2. My na - tive country, thee, Land of the no - ble free, Thy name I love;
3. Our fathers' God! to thee, Author of lib - er - ty, To thee we sing;

Land where my fa - thers died, Land of the pil - grim's pride,
I love thy rocks and rills, Thy woods and tem - pled hills;
Long may our land be bright With free - dom's ho - ly light;

From ev - 'ry mount - ain side Let free - dom ring!
My heart with rapt - ure thrills; Like that a - bove.
Pro - tect us by thy might, Great God, our King!

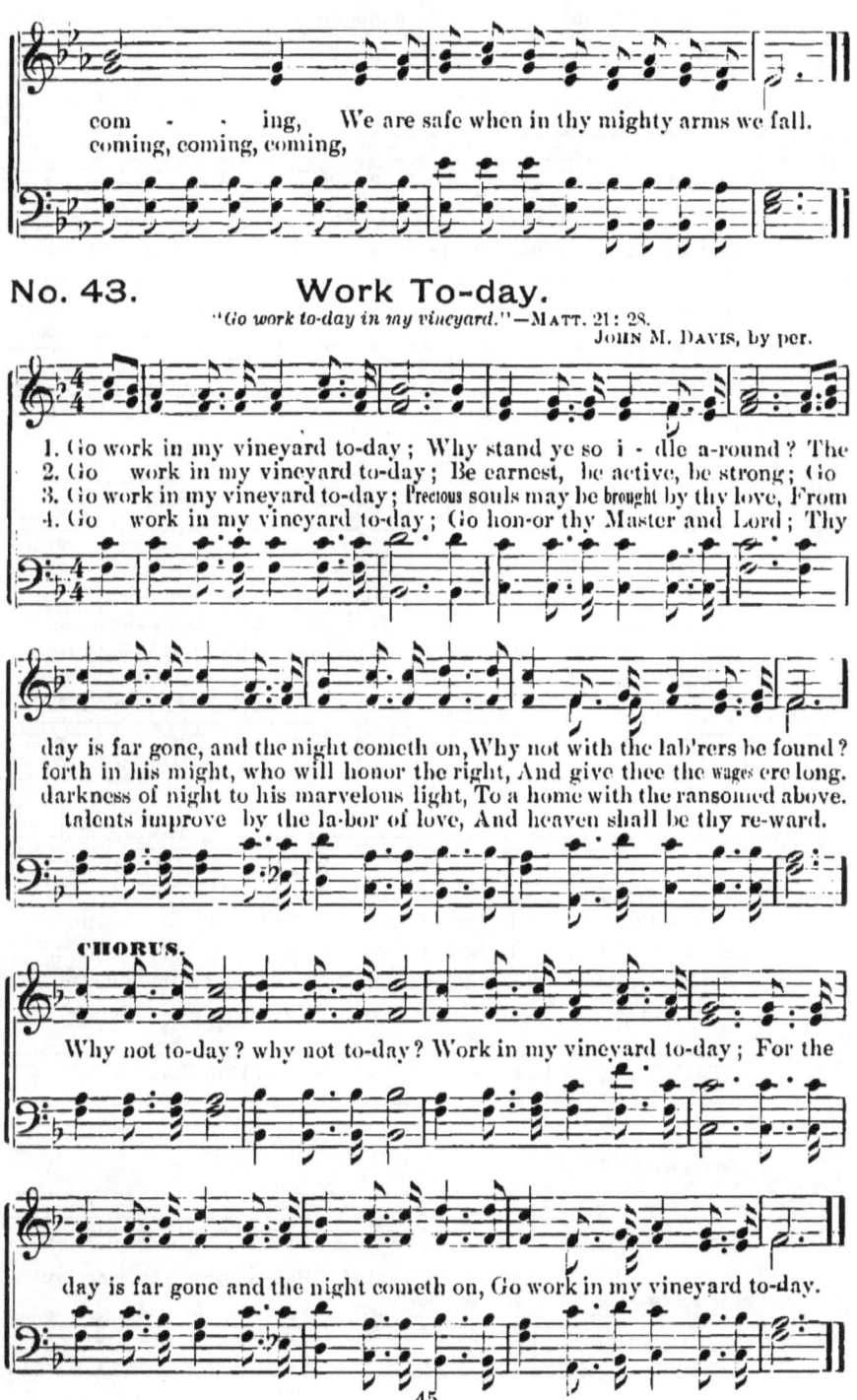

No. 44. Tell It Again.

A home missionary visited a dying boy in a gipsy tent. Bending over him he said: "God so loved the world that he gave his only Son, that whosoever believeth in him should not perish, but have everlasting life. The dying boy heard, and whispered: "Nobody ever told me."

Mrs. M. B. C. SLADE.   R. M. McINTOSH.

1. In-to the tent where a gip-sy boy lay, Dy-ing, a-lone, at the close of the day, News of sal-va-tion we carried—said he: "No-bod-y ev-er has told it to me!"
2. "Did he so love me, a poor lit-tle boy? Send un-to me the good ti-dings of joy? Need I not per-ish?—my hand will he hold?—"No-bod-y ev-er the sto-ry has told."
3. Bending, we caught the last words of his breath, Just as he en-tered the val-ley of death; "God sent his Son!—who-so-ev-er!" said he; "Then I am sure that he sent him for me."
4. Smiling he said, as his last sigh was spent, "I am so glad that for me he was sent!" Whispered while low sank the sun in the west: "Lord, I be-lieve tell it now to the rest."

CHORUS.
Tell it a-gain! tell it a-gain! Sal-va-tion's sto-ry re-

Tell it Again. Concluded.

peat o'er and o'er. Till none can say of the
children of men, "No-bo-dy ev-er has told me be-fore."

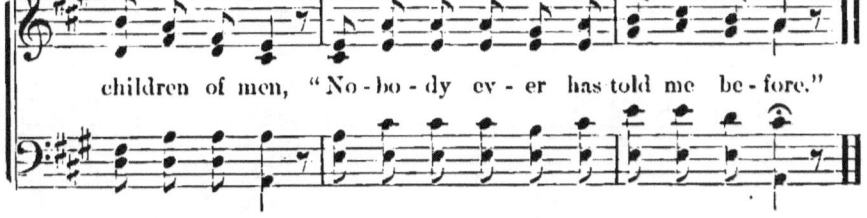

No. 45. Church of God, Awake.

Mrs. EMILY J. BUGBEE. T. C. O'KANE, by per.

1. Church of God, whose conq'ring banners Float along the glorious years,
2. In your costly temples pray-ing, "Let thy kingdom come," we pray,
3. Grace and glory he hath sent you, Cast your line in plac-es fair;
4. Shake the earth and rend the heaven, Wake thy sleeping children, Lord,

Gath'ring har-vest rich and gold-en, Sowed in pov-er-ty and tears:
Are but words of i-dle mean-ing, If with these we turn a-way.
Scat-ter bless-ings now, he bids you, O'er his green earth ev'ry-where.
Till the measure full and e-ven Has been rendered at thy word.

Church of God, Awake. Concluded.

Onward press, the cross is bending Far to-ward the morning skies,
Boundless wealth to you is giv-en, From his hand who owns it all,
Till the millions in the twilight Of the far - off O - rient land,
Then from out her chrism of sorrow Shall the earth redeemed a-rise,

Speedy dawn of light por-tend-ing, Church of God, a-wake! a - rise!
And his eye be - holds in heav-en What ye ren-der back for all.
In the gra-cious morning splendor Of the gospel light shall stand.
And the fair mil-len - nial mor-row Dawn with o - pal tint - ed skies.

CHORUS.

Church of God, . . . awake! a-rise! Christ, your Head and Master,
Church of God, a - wake! a - rise! Christ, your Head and

cries, Send the Gos - pel's joyful sound Un-to earth's remotest bound.
Master, cries, Oh, send the Gos - pel's joyful sound

No. 46. Zion.

Thomas Kelly. 1804. T. Hastings.

1. On the mountain's top appearing, Lo, the sacred herald stands,
Welcome news to Zion bearing, Zion long in hostile hands;
2. Has thy night been long and mournful? Have thy friends unfaithful proved?
Have thy foes been proud and scornful, By the sighs and tears unmoved?
3. God, thy God will now restore thee, He himself appears thy friend,
All thy foes shall flee before thee; Here their boasts and triumphs end;
4. Enemies no more shall trouble; All thy wrongs shall be redressed;
For thy shame thou shalt have double, In thy Maker's favor blest;

Mourning captive, God himself shall loose thy bands,
Cease thy mourning: Zion still is well beloved,
Great Deliverance, Zion's King vouchsafes to send,
All thy conflicts End in everlasting rest,

No. 47. Zion stands with Hills Surrounded.

(Tune above.)   Thomas Kelly. 1806.

1 Zion stands with hills surrounded,
  Zion, kept by power divine;
All her foes shall be confounded,
  Tho' the world in arms combine;
    Happy Zion,
What a favored lot is thine!

2 Every human tie may perish;
  Friend to friend unfaithful prove;
Mothers cease their own to cherish;

Heaven and earth at last remove;
  But no changes
Can attend Jehovah's love.

3 If thy God should show displeasure,
  'T is to save, and not destroy:
If he punish, 't is in measure;
  'T is to rid thee of alloy.
    Be thou patient,
Soon thy grief shall turn to joy.

No. 48. Here am I, send me.

Rev. Dan'l March.   S. M. Brown, by per.

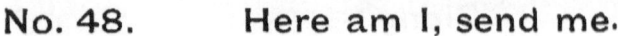

1. Hark! the voice of Jesus crying, "Who will go and work to-day? Fields are white and harvest waiting, Who will bear the sheaves away?" Loud and strong the Master calleth, Rich reward he offers thee; Who will answer, gladly saying, "Here am I; send me, send me"?

2. If you can not cross the ocean, And the heathen lands explore, You can find the heathen nearer, You can help them at your door. If you can not give your thousands, You can give the widow's mite, And the least you do for Jesus, Will be precious in his sight.

3 If you can not speak like angels,
   If you can not preach like Paul,
You can tell the love of Jesus,
   You can say he died for all.
If you can not rouse the wicked
   With the judgment's dread alarms,
You can lead the little children
   To the Savior's waiting arms.

4 If you can not be the watchman,
   Standing high on Zion's wall,
Pointing out the path to heaven,
   Offering life and peace to all;
With your prayers and with your bounties
   You can do what heaven demands;
You can do like faithful Aaron,
   Holding up the prophet's hands.

5 If among the older people,
   You may not be apt to teach;
"Feed my lambs," said Christ, our shepherd,
   "Place the food within their reach."
And it may be that the children
   You have led with trembling hand,
Will be found among your jewels,
   When you reach the better land.

6 Let none hear you idly saying,
   "There is nothing I can do,"
While the souls of men are dying,
   And the Master calls for you.
Take the task he gives you gladly,
   Let his work your pleasure be;
Answer quickly when he calleth,
   "Here am I; send me, send me."

From "Gospel Alarm."

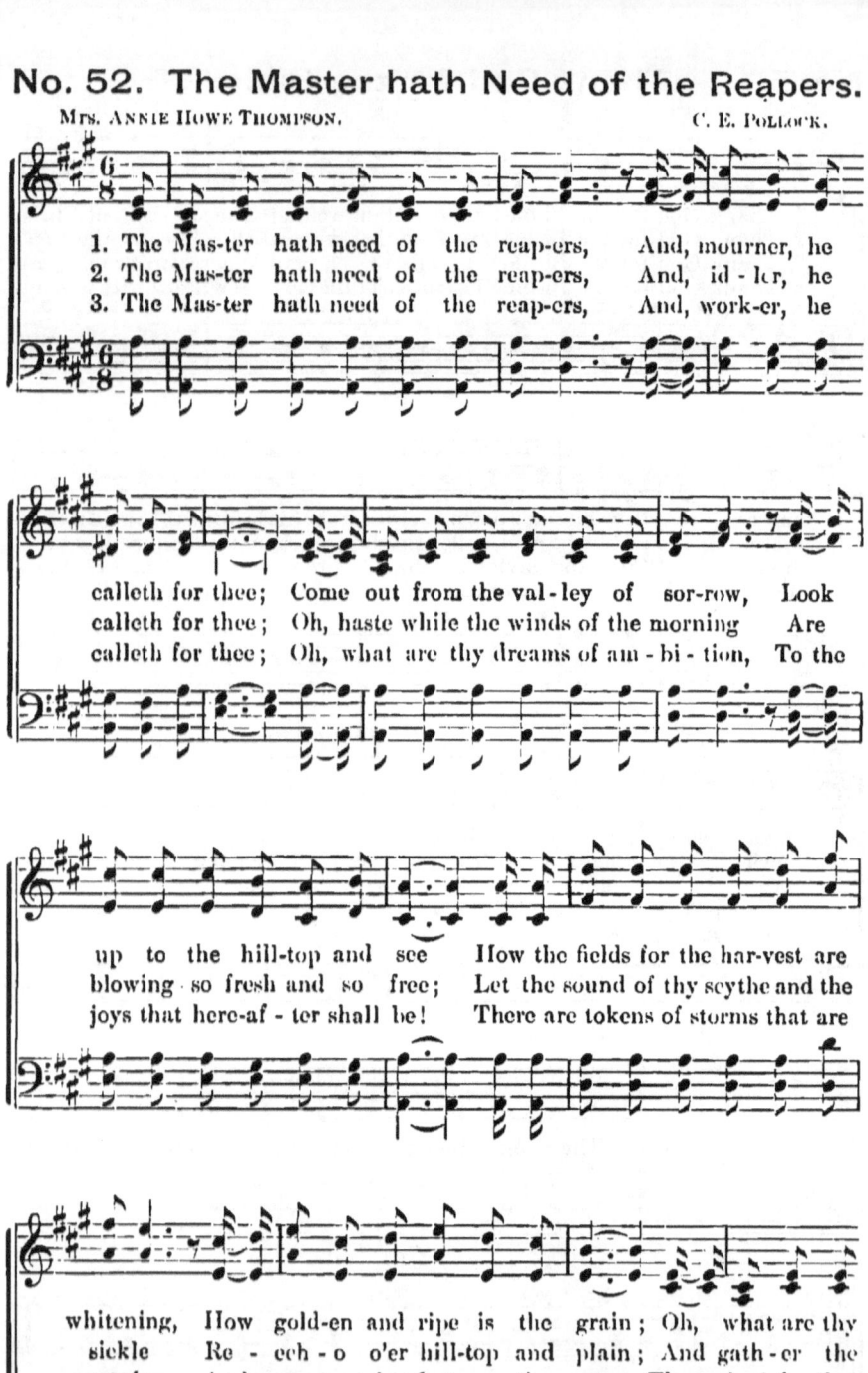

Army of the Lord. Concluded.

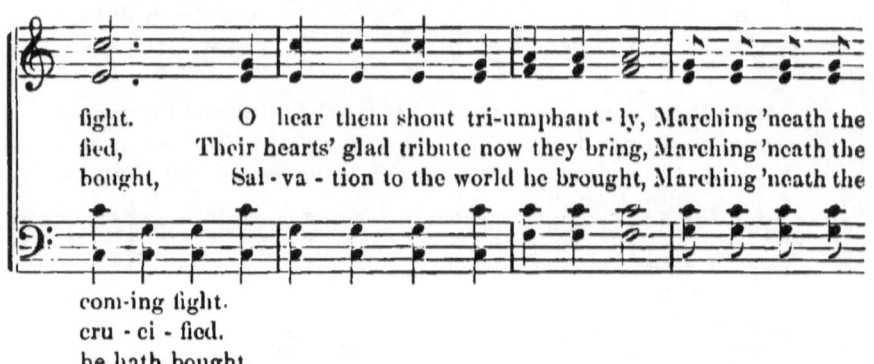

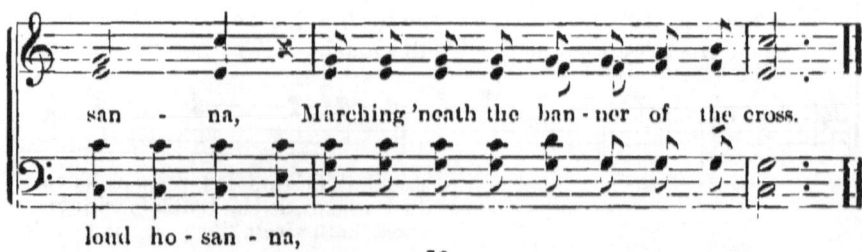

No. 54. Keep the Banner Unfurled.

J. H. LUTHER.   J. M. HUNT, by per.

1. Our country for Je-sus, The land of the free, From o-cean to ocean, From mountain to sea; The Lord is our Captain, His word is our guide, We're on-ly to fol-low, Whate'er may be-tide. Keep the banner un-furled And the vict'ry loud sing, Thus to conquer the world For Jesus our King.

2. Our country for Je-sus, The light of the world; Our triumph is certain, With banner unfurled; For truth is victorious O'er error and race, While love sings melodious The song of free grace.

3. The children are call-ing, Are call-ing for light, While thousands are praying And toiling with might; Then let us be faithful, The harvest is white, The Bridegroom is coming, Our lamps should be bright.

ff CHORUS.

From "Gospel Alarm."

The Bible. Concluded.

Does the word of God afford, Giving life and
Giving life and endless pleasure,

endless pleasure, In the presence of the Lord.
Giving life and endless pleasure,

No. 56. Hebron. L. M.

ISAAC WATTS.   Dr. L. MASON. 1830.

1. Great God, whose universal sway The known and unknown worlds obey;
2. As rain on meadows newly mown, So shall he send his influence down;
3. The heathen lands, that lie beneath The shade of overspreading death,
4. The saints shall flourish in his days, Dressed in the robes of joy and praise;

Now give thy kingdom to thy Son, Extend his power, exalt his throne.
His grace on fainting souls distils Like heavenly dew on thirsty hills.
Revive at his first dawning light, And deserts blossom at the sight.
Peace, like a river, from his throne Shall flow to nations yet unknown.

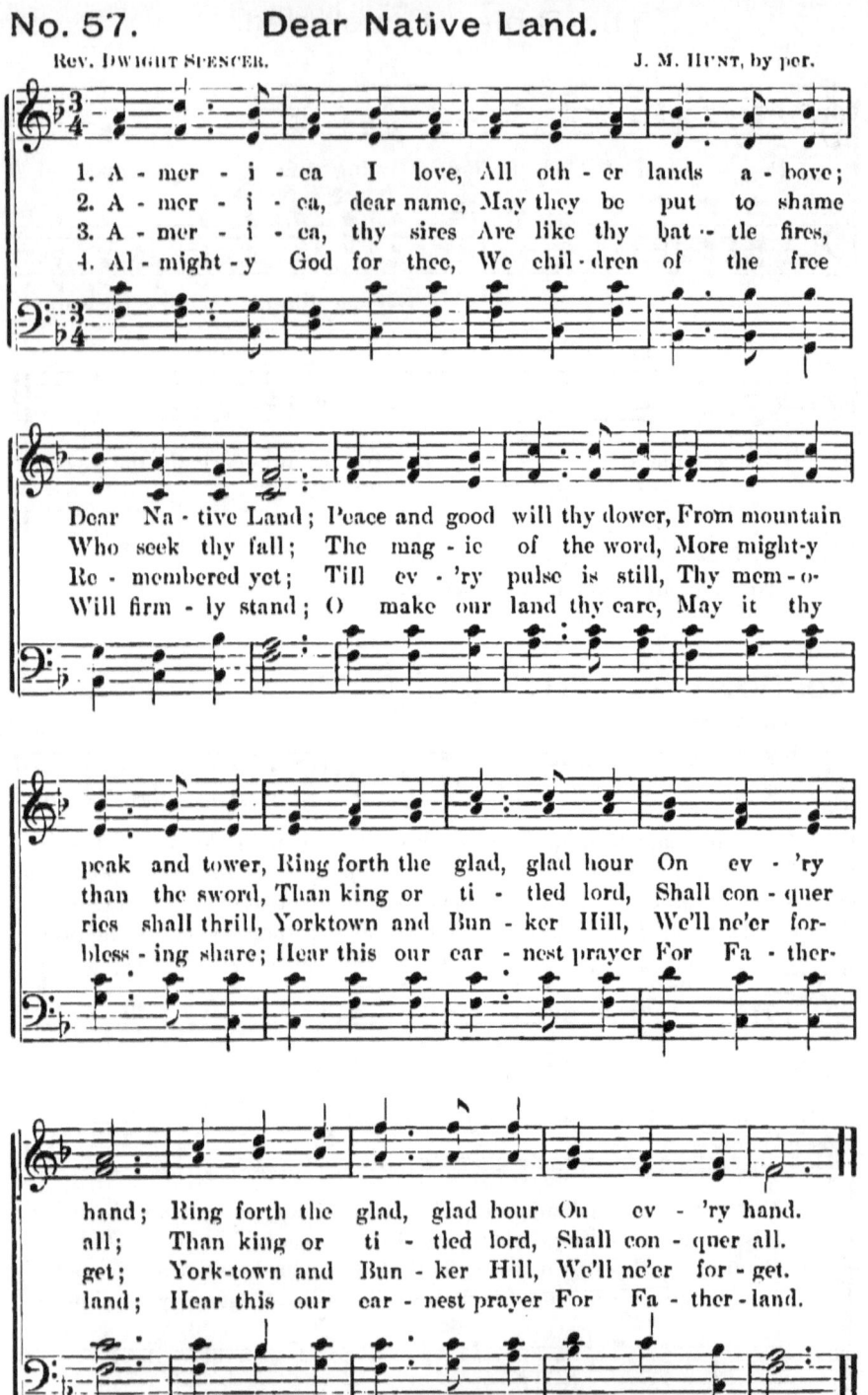

There's a Cry. Concluded.

And the ransomed shall re-turn To the kingdoms of the blest, With their
Till the knowledge of the truth Shall extend to all the earth, As the

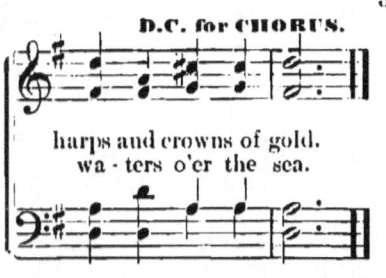

D.C. for CHORUS.

harps and crowns of gold.
wa-ters o'er the sea.

3 Ye have 'listed in the army of the faithful,
    Like heroes the battle fight,
  There are foes on every hand that will assail you,
    Then gird on your armor bright;
  With the banner of the cross unfurled before you,
    The sword of the Spirit wield,
  You shall conquer thro' his mercy who hath loved you,
    The Lord is your strength and shield.
  Ye are marching to the land
  Where the saints in glory stand,
    And the just for joy shall sing;
  Ye by faith may bring it nigh,
  Ye shall reach it by and by,
    And your shouts of triumph ring.

No. 60.   O When shall these Glad Tidings.

J. M. HUNT.

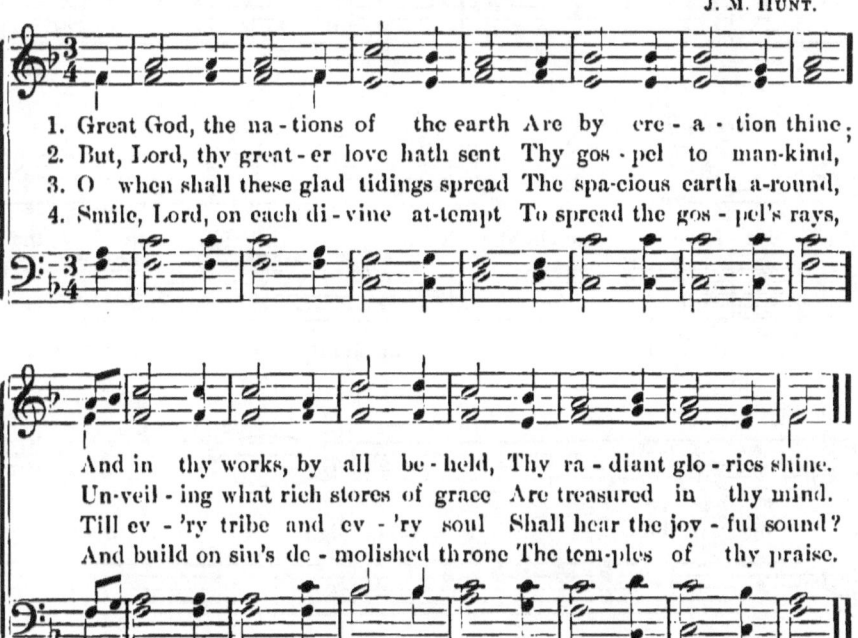

1. Great God, the na-tions of the earth Are by cre-a-tion thine,
2. But, Lord, thy great-er love hath sent Thy gos-pel to man-kind,
3. O when shall these glad tidings spread The spa-cious earth a-round,
4. Smile, Lord, on each di-vine at-tempt To spread the gos-pel's rays,

And in thy works, by all be-held, Thy ra-diant glo-ries shine.
Un-veil-ing what rich stores of grace Are treasured in thy mind.
Till ev-'ry tribe and ev-'ry soul Shall hear the joy-ful sound?
And build on sin's de-molished throne The tem-ples of thy praise.

No. 61. Rejoice and Shout Aloud.

T. E. VASSAR, D.D. ISAAC H. BULLERS.

1. Not yet beneath our Captain's feet Lie sin and death, and pain and woe;
2. Yet, come it shall, and even now Faith views the victo - ry as won;
3. Like bugle blast, rings clear and strong That pledge of prophet, from afar
4. Amen, Lord Jesus, onward sweep; The lingering ages wait the sway,
5. With yearning heart and lifted eye The toilers watch and ever sing,

Not yet the anthem, clear and sweet, Of heaven, above, on earth, below.
All hearts must yield, all knees must bend To God's beloved anointed Son.
He shall not fail to right the wrong, The isles shall speed the conqueror's car.
The scepter stretch o'er land and deep, Bring in the golden noontide day
Thy kingdom, glory, power come nigh, Let hallelu-jahs sweet-ly ring.

CHORUS.

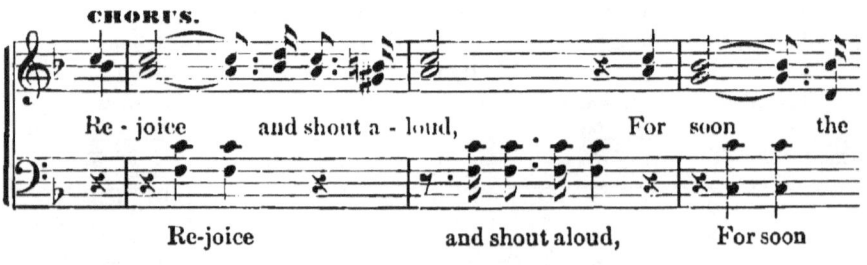

Re - joice and shout a - loud, For soon the
Re-joice and shout aloud, For soon

time will be, When light . . . shall break the
the time will be, When light

Rejoice and Shout Aloud. Concluded.

cloud, When Christ shall reign supreme, eter-nal-ly.

shall break the cloud,

No. 62. The Mighty Song.

EMMA PITT.   J. M. HUNT.

1. Down the column of the a - ges Grandest echoes roll a - long,
2. Ev - er, ev - er still in-creas-ing, Sounding o'er each distant chime,
3. Let us sing our Savior's praises, Tarrying in this un-der clime,

Ev - er in their force increasing, Till the earth is filled with song.
Till our earth e'en up to heav-en Echoes with the hallowed rhyme.
Yonder we will sing ho-san - nas, Measured not by flight of time.

CHORUS.

Clear and sweet the full vibrations Of the mighty, mighty song,

For the grand key-note is Jesus, And it thrills the countless throng.

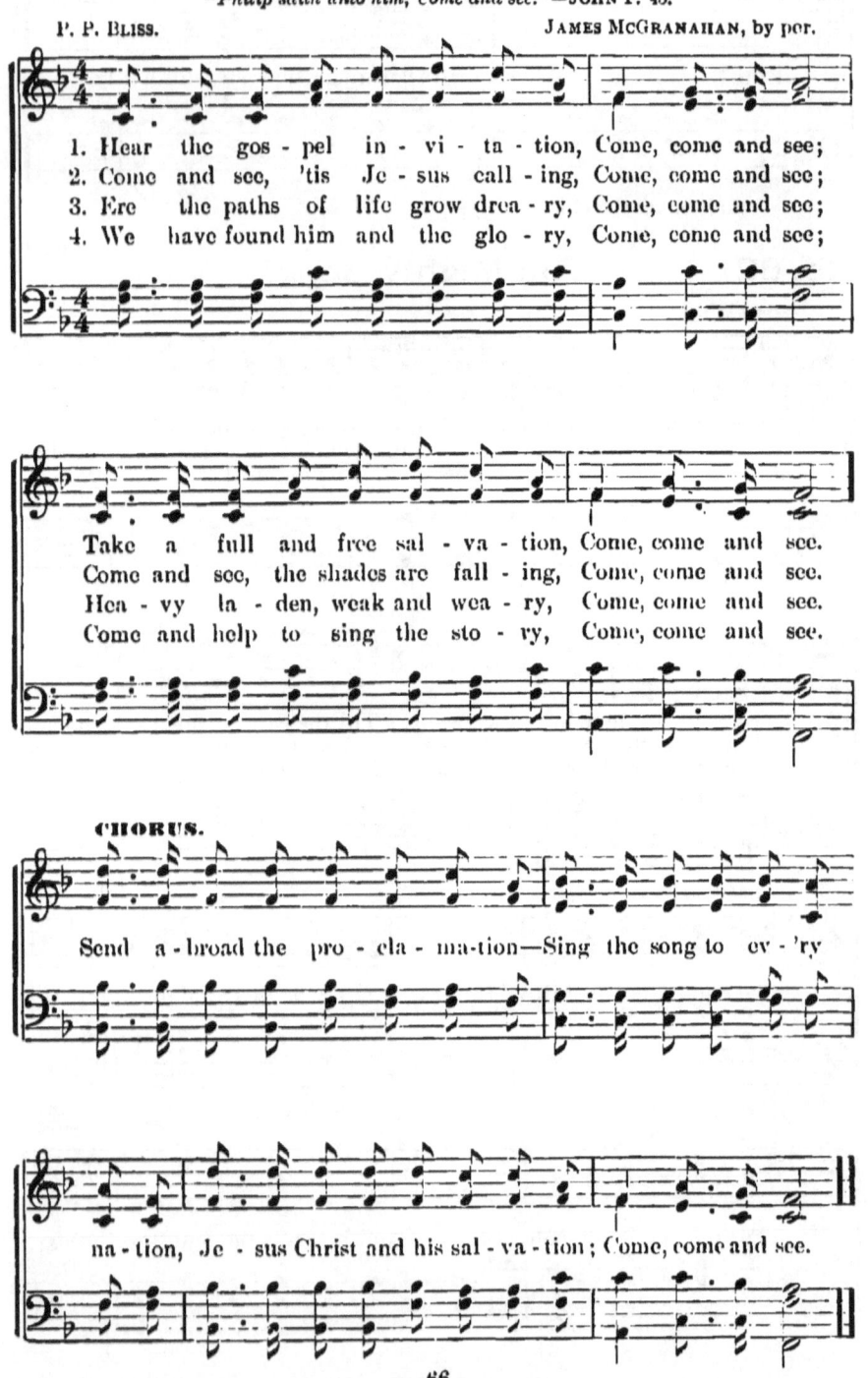

No. 64. Go Work in my Vineyard.

"Why stand ye here all the day idle." —MATT. 20. 6.

From "Missionary Helper." J. R. MURRAY, by per.

1. Speak some word, where'er thou roamest, For the Lord of Love;
2. Where the sweet young child is playing In the frond-ed grove;
3. Where the skep-tic—bold and scornful, Makes his wi-ly plea,

For that word may find an ech-o In the world a-bove.
Go and tell the wondrous sto-ry Of our Sav-ior's love.
There they need to learn of Je-sus— There is work for thee.

Go where hearts are dai-ly bow-ing To some i-dol shrine;
Where the heart is held in fet-ters By the cru-el bowl,
Go, then, work as Christ shall bid thee, Wait not till the night;

Tell them God a-lone will hear them, He is all di-vine.
Go to them with gen-tle plead-ing, Love may win the soul.
Tho' the prospect may be gloom-y, Christ shall give thee light.

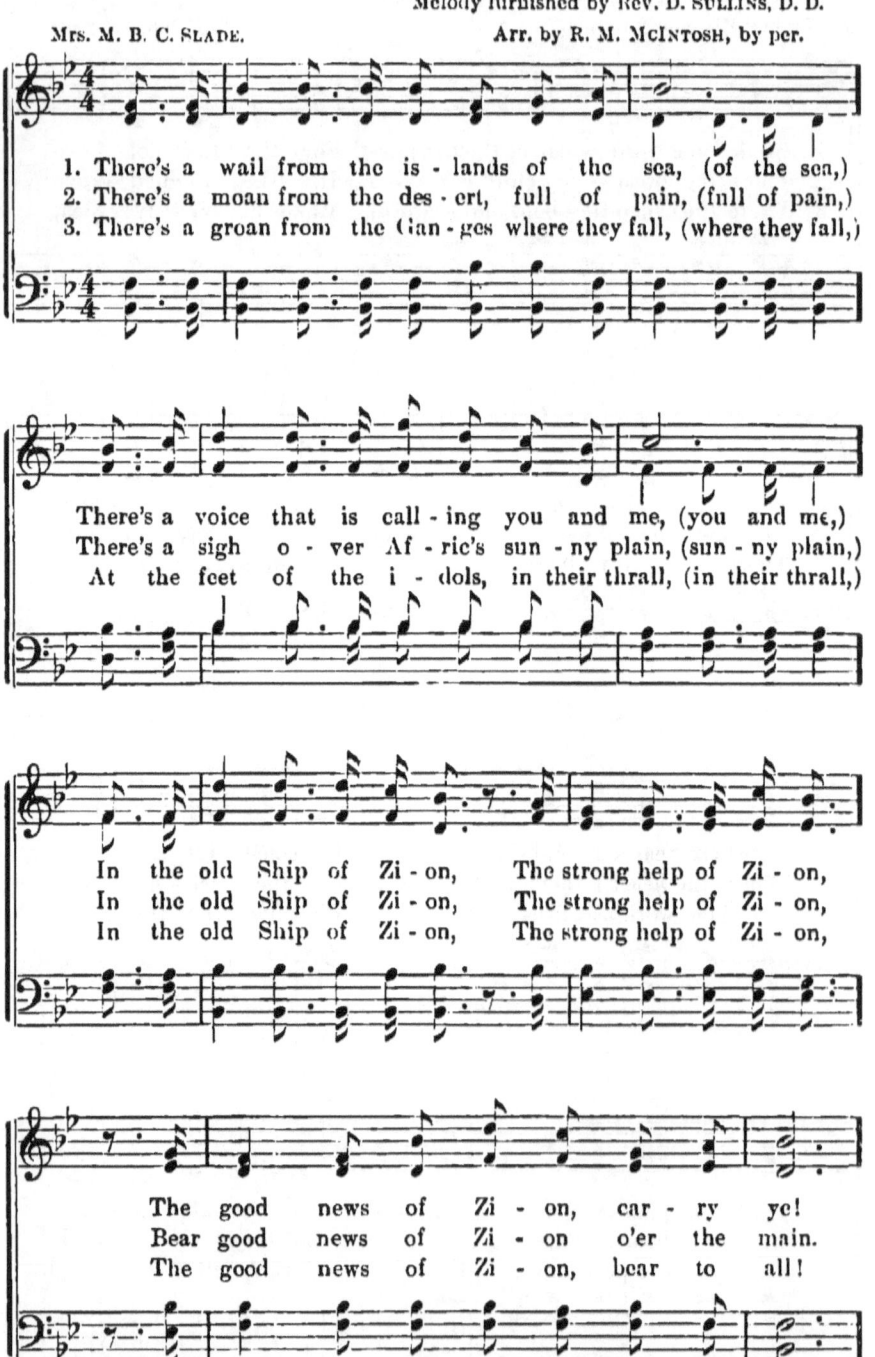

Ship of Zion. Concluded.

69

Ring the Bells. Concluded.

Je-sus has ris'n the lost to save; Ring, ring the bells, the sweet Gospel bells.

No. 67. Christ for the World.

S. WALCOTT.   CHAS. EDW. POLLOCK.

1. Christ for the world, we sing; The world to Christ we bring With lov - ing zeal; The poor and them that mourn, The faint and o - ver-borne, Sin - sick and sor - row-worn, Whom Christ doth heal.
2. Christ for the world, we sing; The world to Christ we bring With fer - vent prayer; The way-ward and the lost, By rest - less passions tossed, Re-deemed at countless cost From dark de - spair.
3. Christ for the world, we sing; The world to Christ we bring With one ac - cord; With us the work to share, With us re-proach to dare, With us the cross to bear For Christ, our Lord.
4. Christ for the world, we sing; The world to Christ we bring With joy - ful song; The new-born soul whose days Reclaimed from er - ror's ways, In-spired with hope and praise, To Christ be - long.

The Light of the World. Concluded.

Once I was blind, but now I can see; The Light of the world is Je-sus.

No. 69.   **Kedesh.**

Dr. L. MASON.

1. Yes, my native land, I love thee; All thy scenes, I love them well;
2. Home, thy joys are passing lovely—Joys no strang-er heart can tell;

Friends, connections, hap-py coun-try, Can I bid you all farewell?
Happy home, in-deed I love thee, Can I, can I say, "Farewell?"

Can I leave you, Can I leave you, Far in heath-en lands to dwell?
Can I leave you, Can I leave you, Far in heath-en lands to dwell?

3 Scenes of sacred peace and pleasure,
Holy days and Sabbath bell,
Richest, brightest, sweetest treasure,
Can I say a last farewell?
Can I leave you, Can I leave you,
Far in heathen lands to dwell?

4 Yes, I hasten from you gladly,
From the scenes I loved so well;
Far away, ye billows, bear me;
Lovely native land, farewell!
Pleased I leave thee, Pleased I leave thee,
Far in heathen lands to dwell.

5 In the deserts let me labor;
On the mountains let me tell
How he died—the blessed Savior—
To redeem a world from hell:
Let me hasten, Let me hasten,
Far in heathen lands to dwell.

6 Bear me on, thou restless ocean;
Let the winds my canvas swell;
Heaves my heart with warm emotion,
While I go far hence to dwell;
Glad I bid thee, Glad I bid thee,
Native land, farewell, farewell!

Every One to the Work. Concluded.

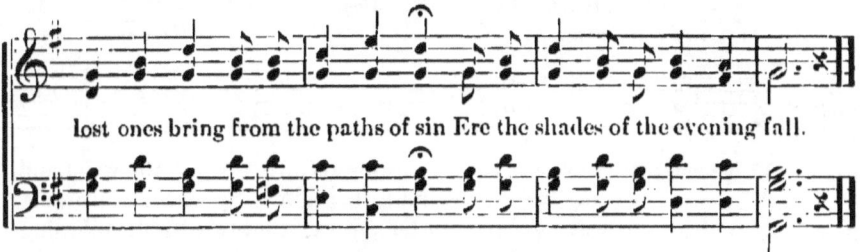

lost ones bring from the paths of sin Ere the shades of the evening fall.

No. 71. Dear Children far Away.

"*Such as sit in darkness, and in the shadow of death.*"—Ps. 107: 10.

J. R. MURRAY, by per.

1. In lands full of dark-ness a-cross the blue wave, Are ma-ny dear
2. No kind Christian pa-rents to show them the way, To tell them of
3. No Bi-ble to brighten their path-way of gloom, No hope full of
4. No Je-sus, no Bi-ble—how sad is the sight, While here o'er our

chil-dren the Lord died to save; Who, reaching out hands from far
Je-sus, to teach them to pray; To lead them in path-ways of
glo-ry be-yond the dark tomb; No prom-ise of God the sad
pathway the gos-pel shines bright; Lord, o-pen our hearts to the

o-ver the sea, Are pleading for light shin-ing on us so free.
wisdom and truth, And teach them the love of our God in their youth.
soul to sus-tain, No knowledge that death to the Christian is gain.
poor children there, To give them the Bi-ble, our help and our pray'r.

The Word of Life. Concluded.

A - way o'er the o - cean wave, A - way to the woodland deep,
ocean wave, woodland deep,
A - way, a - way with the "Word of Life," Where boundless prairies sweep.

No. 73. Jesus shall Reign.

ISAAC WATTS. 1719. J. M. HUNT.

1. Jesus shall reign where'er the sun Does his successive journeys run;
2. For him shall endless prayer be made, And praises throng to crown his head;
3. People and realms of every tongue Dwell on his love with sweetest song;
4. Blessings abound where'er he reigns; The prisoner leaps to lose his chains;
5. Let every creature rise and bring Pe - culiar hon-ors to our King;

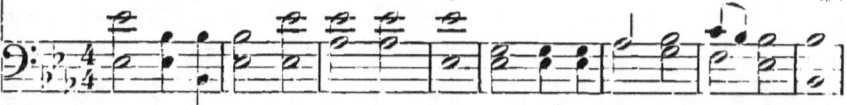

His kingdom stretch from shore to shore, Till moons shall wax and wane no more.
His name like sweet perfume shall rise With every morning sac - ri - fice.
And infant voic-es shall proclaim Their early blessings on his name.
The weary find e - ter - nal rest, And all the sons of want are blest.
Angels descend with songs a-gain, And earth repeat the loud A-men!

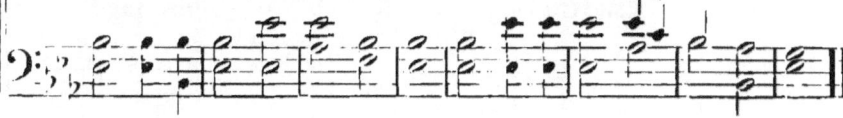

No. 74.   Hunt.

R. HEBER.   Written for this work.   CHAS. EDW. POLLOCK.

Spirited.

1. From Greenland's ic-y mountains, From India's cor-al strand, Where Af-ric's sun-ny fount-ains Roll down their gold-en sand; From many an an-cient riv-er, From many a palm-y plain, They call us to de-liv-er Their land from er-ror's chain.

2. What tho' the spic-y breez-es Blow soft o'er Ceylon's isle, Tho' ev-'ry pro-spect pleas-es, And on-ly man is vile! In vain, with lav-ish kind-ness, The gifts of God are strown; The heath-en, in his blind-ness, Bows down to wood and stone.

3. Can we, whose souls are light-ed By wis-dom from on high, Can we, to men be-night-ed, The lamp of life de-ny? Sal-va-tion! oh, sal-va-tion! The joy-ful sound pro-claim, Till earth's re-mot-est na-tion Has learned Mes-si-ah's name.

4. Waft, waft, ye winds, his sto-ry, And you, ye wa-ters, roll, Till, like a sea of glo-ry, It spreads from pole to pole; Till, o'er our ran-somed nat-ure, The Lamb for sin-ners slain, Re-deem-er, King, Cre-a-tor, In bliss re-turns to reign.

No. 75. Blow ye the Trumpet.

"Then shalt thou cause the trumpet of the jubilee to sound." — LEV. 25: 9.

CHAS. WESLEY.   EDSON.

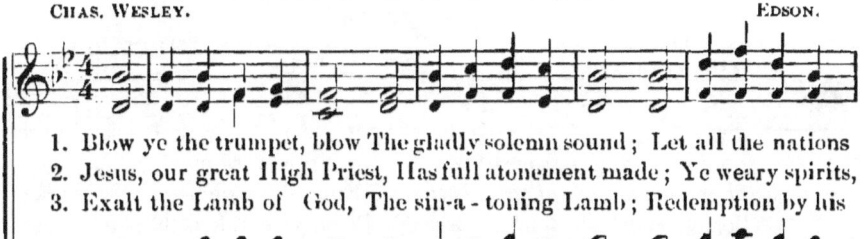

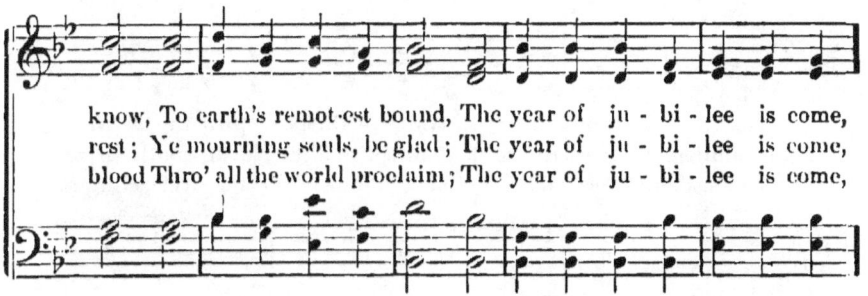

1. Blow ye the trumpet, blow The gladly solemn sound; Let all the nations know, To earth's remotest bound, The year of ju-bi-lee is come, The year of ju-bi-lee is come; Return, ye ransom'd sin-ners, home.
2. Jesus, our great High Priest, Has full atonement made; Ye weary spirits, rest; Ye mourning souls, be glad; The year of ju-bi-lee is come,
3. Exalt the Lamb of God, The sin-a-toning Lamb; Redemption by his blood Thro' all the world proclaim; The year of ju-bi-lee is come,

No. 76. Arise, my Soul, Arise.

(Tune above.)

1 Arise, my soul, arise;
   Shake off thy guilty fears,
The bleeding sacrifice
   In my behalf appears;
Before the throne my surety stands,
My name is written on his hands.

2 He ever lives above,
   For me to intercede,
His all-redeeming love,
   His precious blood to plead;
His blood atoned for all our race,
And sprinkles now the throne of grace.

3 My God is reconciled;
   His pardoning voice I hear;
He owns me for his child,
   I can no longer fear;
With confidence I now draw nigh,
And Father, Abba, Father, cry.

Shout for Gladness. Concluded.

No. 78. Watchman, Tell Me.

"*Watchman, what of the night.*"—ISA. 21: 11.

Rev. SIDNEY S. BREWER. WM. B. BRADBURY, by per.

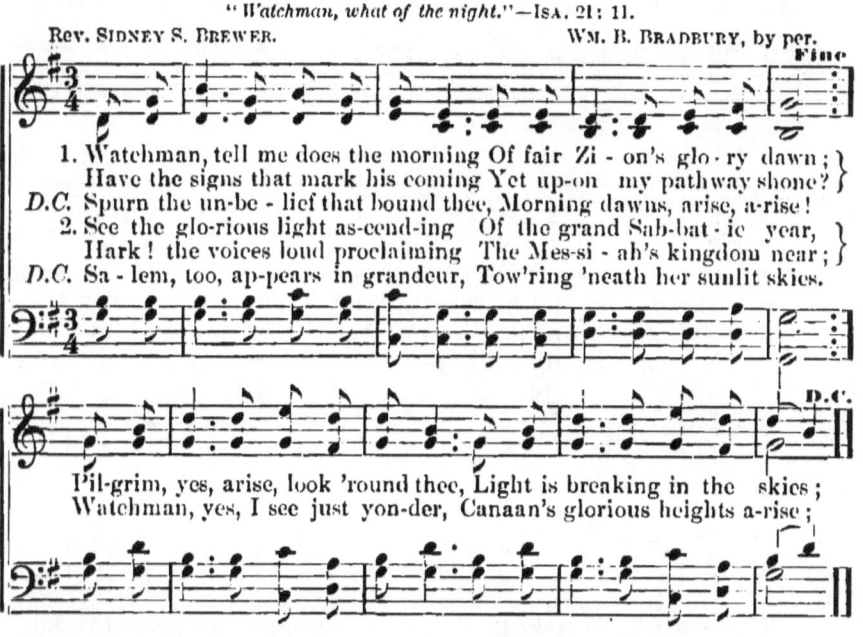

3 Pilgrim, in that golden city,
  Seated in the jasper throne,
Zion's King, arrayed in beauty,
  Reigns in peace from zone to zone;
There, on verdant hills and mountains,
  Where the golden sunbeams play,
Purling streams, and crystal fountains,
  Sparkle in th' eternal day.

4 Pilgrim, see! the light is beaming
  Brighter still upon the way;
Signs thro' all the earth are gleaming,
  Omens of the coming day.
When the last loud trumpet sounding,
  Shall awake from earth to sea
All the saints of God now sleeping—
  Clad in immortality.

No. 79. Go and Labor.

CHAS. H. GABRIEL. J. M. HUNT.

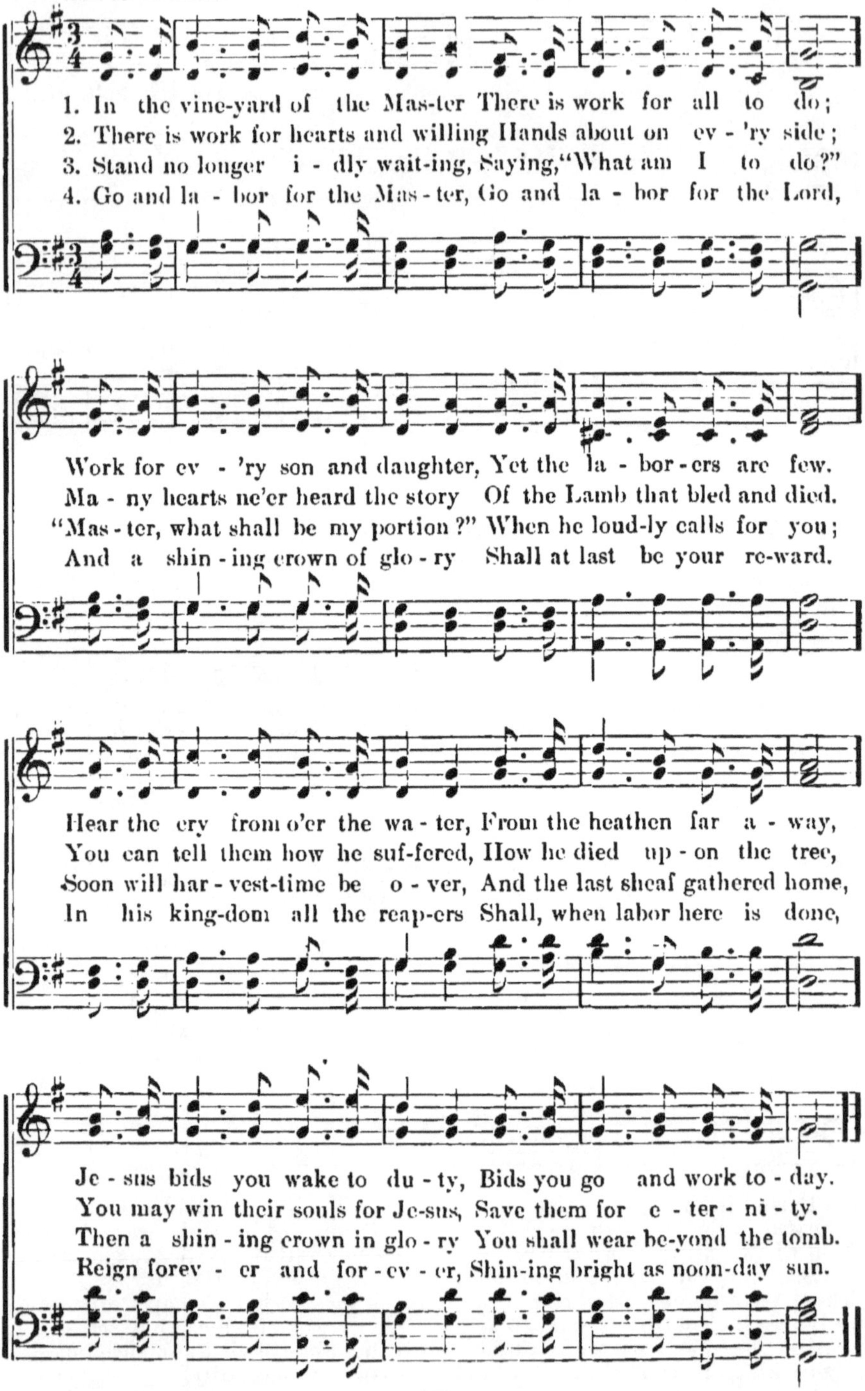

1. In the vine-yard of the Mas-ter There is work for all to do;
2. There is work for hearts and willing Hands about on ev-'ry side;
3. Stand no longer i-dly wait-ing, Saying,"What am I to do?"
4. Go and la-bor for the Mas-ter, Go and la-bor for the Lord,

Work for ev-'ry son and daughter, Yet the la-bor-ers are few.
Ma-ny hearts ne'er heard the story Of the Lamb that bled and died.
"Mas-ter, what shall be my portion?" When he loud-ly calls for you;
And a shin-ing crown of glo-ry Shall at last be your re-ward.

Hear the cry from o'er the wa-ter, From the heathen far a-way,
You can tell them how he suf-fered, How he died up-on the tree,
Soon will har-vest-time be o-ver, And the last sheaf gathered home,
In his king-dom all the reap-ers Shall, when labor here is done,

Je-sus bids you wake to du-ty, Bids you go and work to-day.
You may win their souls for Je-sus, Save them for e-ter-ni-ty.
Then a shin-ing crown in glo-ry You shall wear be-yond the tomb.
Reign forev-er and for-ev-er, Shin-ing bright as noon-day sun.

No. 80.   Duke Street.
HATTON.

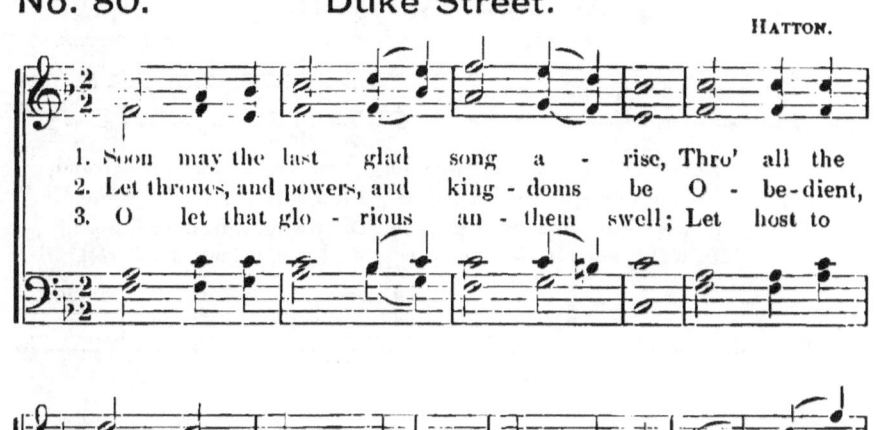

1. Soon may the last glad song a-rise, Thro' all the
2. Let thrones, and powers, and king-doms be O-be-dient,
3. O let that glo-rious an-them swell; Let host to

mil - lions of the skies—That song of tri - umph
might - y God, to thee; And o - ver land, and
host the tri - umph tell, Till not one reb - el

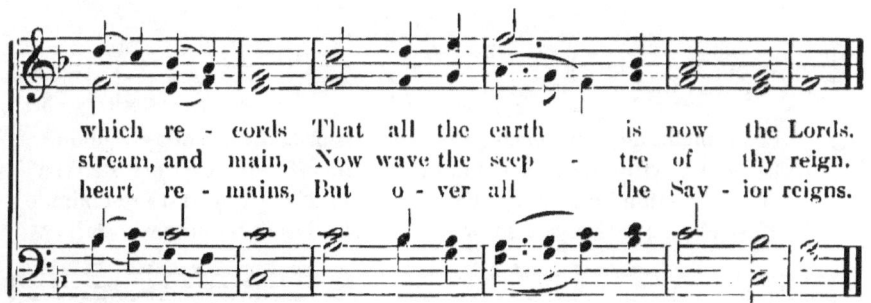

which re - cords That all the earth is now the Lord's.
stream, and main, Now wave the scep - tre of thy reign.
heart re - mains, But o - ver all the Sav - ior reigns.

No. 81.   Ye Nations of the Earth.
(Tune above.)

1 Ye nations round the earth, rejoice
  Before the Lord, your sovereign King,
Serve him with cheerful heart and voice,
  With all your tongues his glory sing.

2 The Lord is God, 'tis he alone
  Doth life and breath and being give;
We are his work, and not our own;
  The sheep that on his pastures live.

3 Enter his gates with songs of joy,
  With praises to his courts repair,
And make it your divine employ
  To pay your thanks and honors there.

4 The Lord is good; the Lord is kind;
  Great is his grace, his mercy sure;
And the whole race of man shall find
  His truth from age to age endure.

No. 82. Missionary Hymn.

HEBER. Dr. L. MASON.

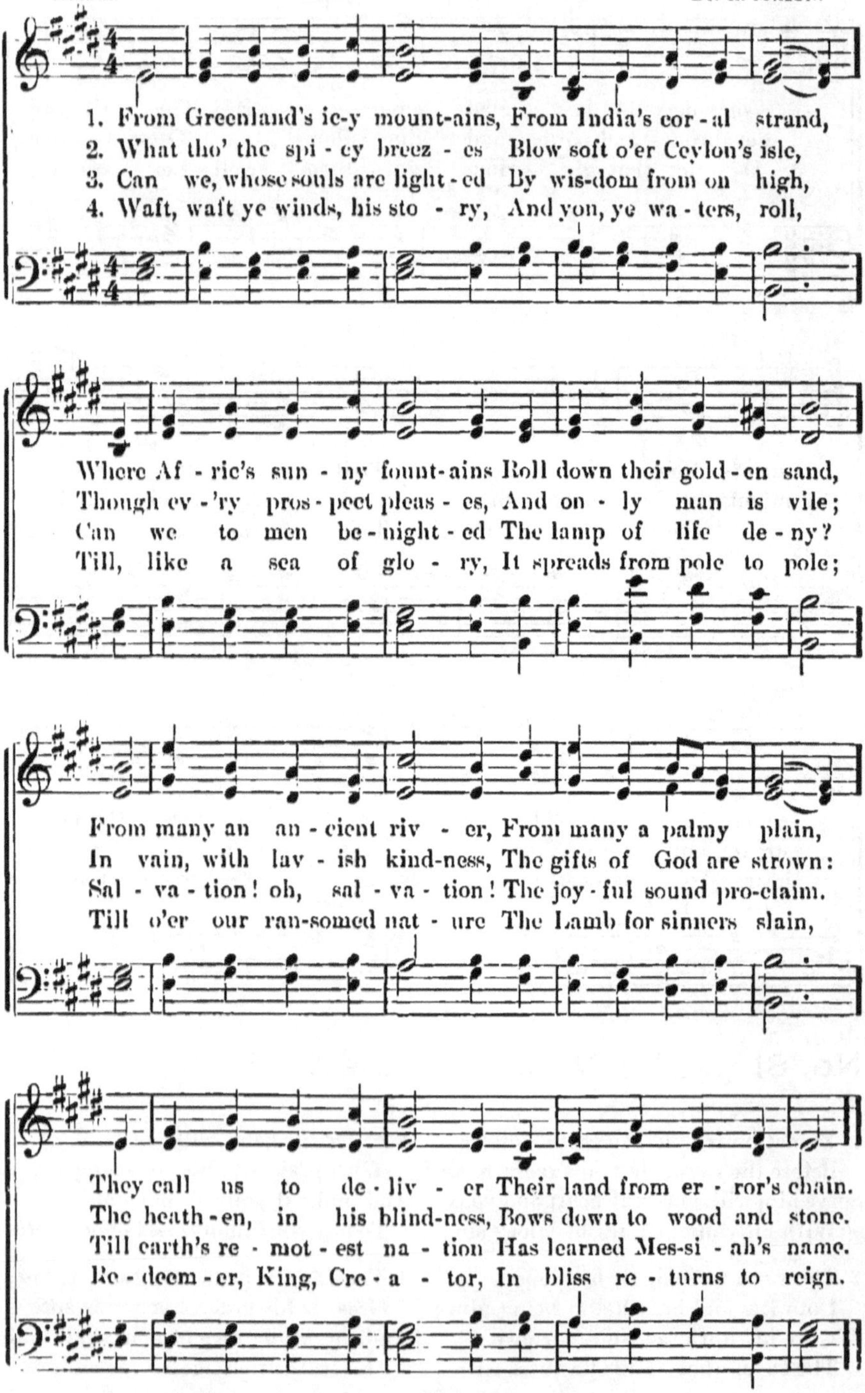

1. From Greenland's ic-y mount-ains, From India's cor-al strand,
2. What tho' the spi-cy breez-es Blow soft o'er Ceylon's isle,
3. Can we, whose souls are light-ed By wis-dom from on high,
4. Waft, waft ye winds, his sto-ry, And you, ye wa-ters, roll,

Where Af-ric's sun-ny fount-ains Roll down their gold-en sand,
Though ev-'ry pros-pect pleas-es, And on-ly man is vile;
Can we to men be-night-ed The lamp of life de-ny?
Till, like a sea of glo-ry, It spreads from pole to pole;

From many an an-cient riv-er, From many a palmy plain,
In vain, with lav-ish kind-ness, The gifts of God are strown:
Sal-va-tion! oh, sal-va-tion! The joy-ful sound pro-claim.
Till o'er our ran-somed nat-ure The Lamb for sinners slain,

They call us to de-liv-er Their land from er-ror's chain.
The heath-en, in his blind-ness, Bows down to wood and stone.
Till earth's re-mot-est na-tion Has learned Mes-si-ah's name.
Re-deem-er, King, Cre-a-tor, In bliss re-turns to reign.

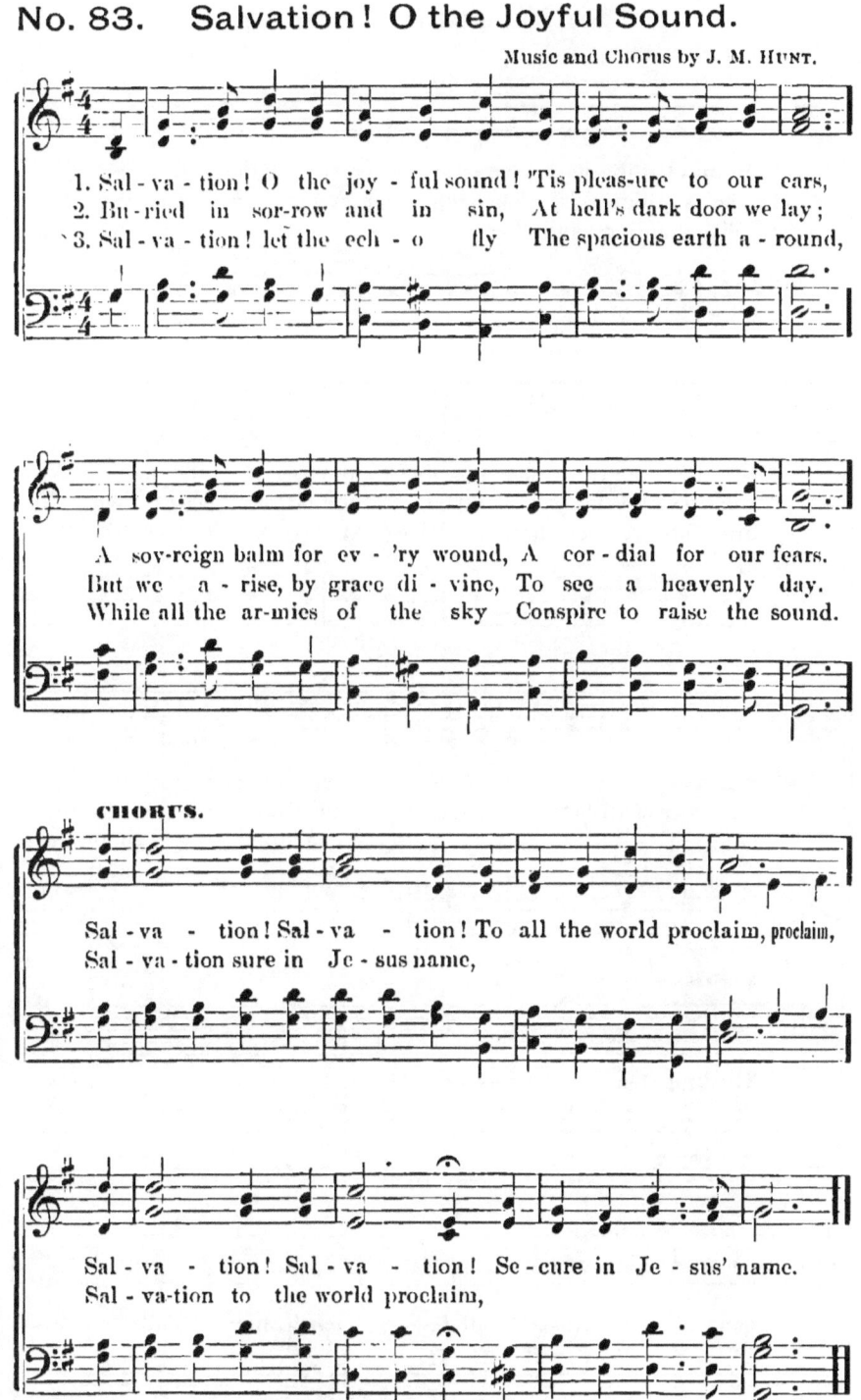

No. 83. Salvation! O the Joyful Sound.

Music and Chorus by J. M. HUNT.

1. Salvation! O the joyful sound! 'Tis pleasure to our ears,
A sov'reign balm for ev'ry wound, A cordial for our fears.

2. Buried in sorrow and in sin, At hell's dark door we lay;
But we arise, by grace divine, To see a heavenly day.

3. Salvation! let the echo fly The spacious earth around,
While all the armies of the sky Conspire to raise the sound.

CHORUS.

Salvation! Salvation! To all the world proclaim, proclaim,
Salvation sure in Jesus name.

Salvation! Salvation! Secure in Jesus' name.
Salvation to the world proclaim,

No. 84. The Kingdom Coming.

Mrs. M. B. C. Slade.   R. M. McIntosh, by per.

1. From all the dark plac-es Of earth's heathen rac-es Oh, see how the thick shadows fly! The voice of sal-va-tion A-wakes ev-'ry na-tion; Come o-ver and help us, they cry.
2. The sun-light is glanc-ing O'er ar-mies ad-vanc-ing To con-quer the king-dom of sin; Our Lord shall possess them, His pres-ence shall bless them, His beau-ty shall en-ter there-in.
3. With shouting and sing-ing, And ju-bi-lant ring-ing, Their arms of re-bel-lion cast down; At last ev-'ry na-tion The Lord of sal-va-tion Their King and Re-deem-er shall crown.

CHORUS.

The king-dom is com-ing: Oh, tell ye the sto-ry! God's ban-ner ex-alt-ed shall be! The earth shall be full of his

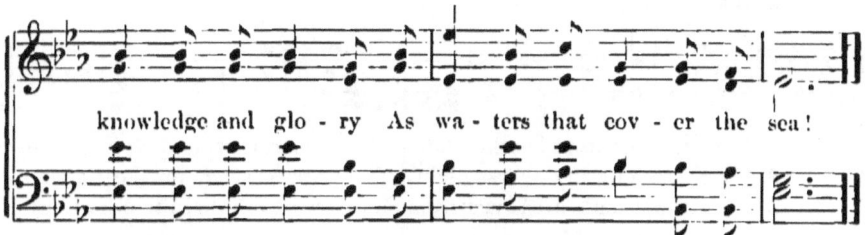

The Kingdom Coming. Concluded.

knowledge and glo-ry As wa-ters that cov-er the sea!

No. 85. Antioch.

Words by WATTS. HANDEL.

1. Joy to the world, the Lord is come! Let earth receive her King! Let
2. Joy to the earth, the Saviour reigns, Let men their songs employ; While
3. No more let sin and sor-row grow, Nor thorns infest the ground; He
4. He rules the world with truth and grace, And makes the nations prove The

ev-'ry heart pre-pare him room, And heav'n and nature sing, And
fields and floods, rocks, hills and plains Re-peat the sounding joy, Re-
comes to make his blessings flow Far as the curse is found, Far
glo-ries of his righteous-ness, And wonders of his love, And

heav'n and na-ture sing, and heav'n, And heav'n and na-ture sing.
peat the sound-ing joy, re-peat, Re-peat the sounding joy.
as the curse is found, far as, Far as the curse is found.
wonders of his love, and won- And won-ders of his love.

No. 86. Hear the Cry.

J. M. Hunt. J. M. Hunt.

1. Hear the cry from heathen lands, As they stretch their helpless hands;
2. Na-tions, long in darkest night, Now are seeking for the light;
3. We, whose souls are saved from sin, Now should help to others win;

Hearken to this plaintive cry, Send the gospel ere they die.
Glad they hear the gospel sound, To the earth's re-mo-test bound.
Jesus pleads and an-gels sing, Shall we not our trophies bring.

CHORUS.

Bear the glad news to every land, Jesus will save with his own hand;

Tell to the lost from shore to shore, Jesus will save for ev-er-more.

No. 87.   Webb.

S. F. SMITH.   G. J. WEBB.

1. The morning light is breaking; The darkness disappears; The sons of earth are
2. See heathen nations bending Before the God we love, And thousand hearts as-
3. Blest riv-er of sal-va-tion, Pursue thy onward way; Flow thou to every

wak-ing To pen-i-tential tears; Each breeze that sweeps the ocean Brings
cend-ing In grat-i-tude a-bove; While sinners, now confessing, The
na-tion, Nor in thy richness stay; Stay not till all the low-ly Tri-

tidings from a-far   Of nations in commotion, Prepared for Zion's war.
gospel call o-bey, And seek the Savior's blessing, A nation in a day.
umphant reach their home; Stay not till all the holy Proclaim, "The Lord is come!"

No. 88.   Stand up for Jesus.
(Tune above.)

1 Stand up! stand up for Jesus!
  Ye soldiers of the cross;
  Lift high his royal banner,
  It must not suffer loss:
  From victory unto victory
  His army shall be led,
  Till every foe is vanquished,
  And Christ is Lord indeed.

2 Stand up! stand up for Jesus!
  Stand in his strength alone;
  The arm of flesh will fail you,
  Ye dare not trust your own :

Put on the gospel armor,
  And watching unto prayer,
  Where duty calls or danger,
  Be never wanting there.

3 Stand up! stand up for Jesus!
  The strife will not be long,
  This day the noise of battle,
  The next the victor's song:
  To him that overcometh,
  A crown of life shall be:
  He with the King of glory
  Shall reign eternally.

No. 89. Crown Him.

Mrs. E. O. Page.   C. C. Case, by per.

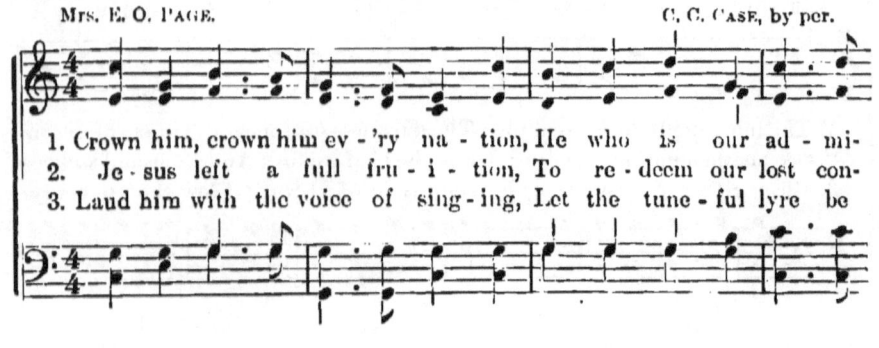

1. Crown him, crown him ev-'ry na-tion, He who is our ad-mi-
2. Jesus left a full fru-i-tion, To re-deem our lost con-
3. Laud him with the voice of sing-ing, Let the tune-ful lyre be

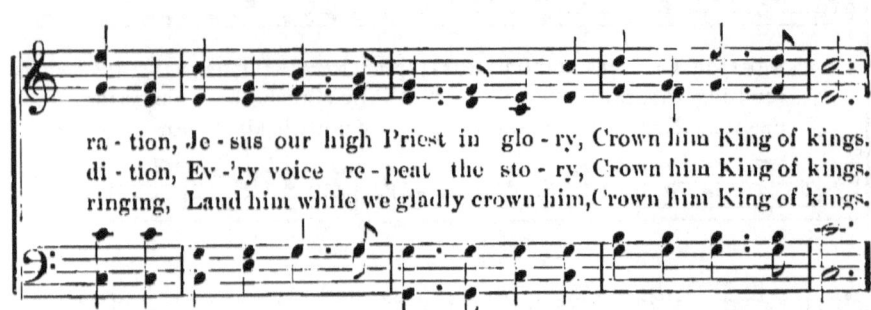

ra-tion, Jesus our high Priest in glo-ry, Crown him King of kings.
di-tion, Ev-'ry voice re-peat the sto-ry, Crown him King of kings.
ringing, Laud him while we gladly crown him, Crown him King of kings.

CHORUS.
Crown him King!

Crown him King of kings!   Loud anthems to his
King of kings,

Crown him King,

glo-ry, Let the na-tions raise.   Crown him King of

Crown Him. Concluded.

kings,. And let the heavens re-peat the sound-ing praise.
King of kings,

No. 90. Form Your Mission Bands.
(Suitable before the collection.)

HEZEKIAH BUTTERWORTH. G. F. ROOT, by per.

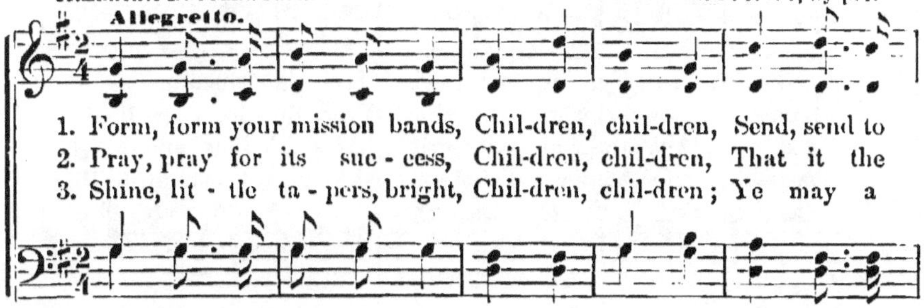

Allegretto.

1. Form, form your mission bands, Chil-dren, chil-dren, Send, send to
2. Pray, pray for its suc - cess, Chil-dren, chil-dren, That it the
3. Shine, lit - tle ta - pers, bright, Chil-dren, chil-dren; Ye may a

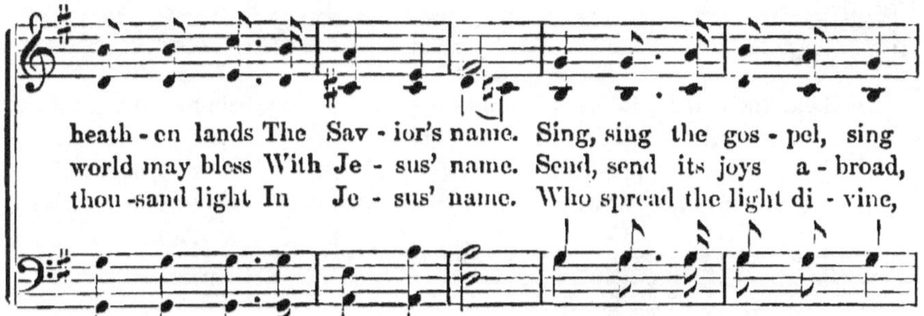

heath - en lands The Sav - ior's name. Sing, sing the gos - pel, sing
world may bless With Je - sus' name. Send, send its joys a - broad,
thou-sand light In Je - sus' name. Who spread the light di - vine,

Chil-dren, chil-dren, Till 'round the world shall ring The Savior's name.
Chil-dren, chil-dren, Give, give the gold of God For Je - sus' name.
Chil-dren, chil-dren, They as the stars shall shine For ev - er - more.

No. 91. Bring Ye in the Tithes.

REV. DWIGHT SPENCER.   MAL. 3: 10.   S. M. BROWN, by per.

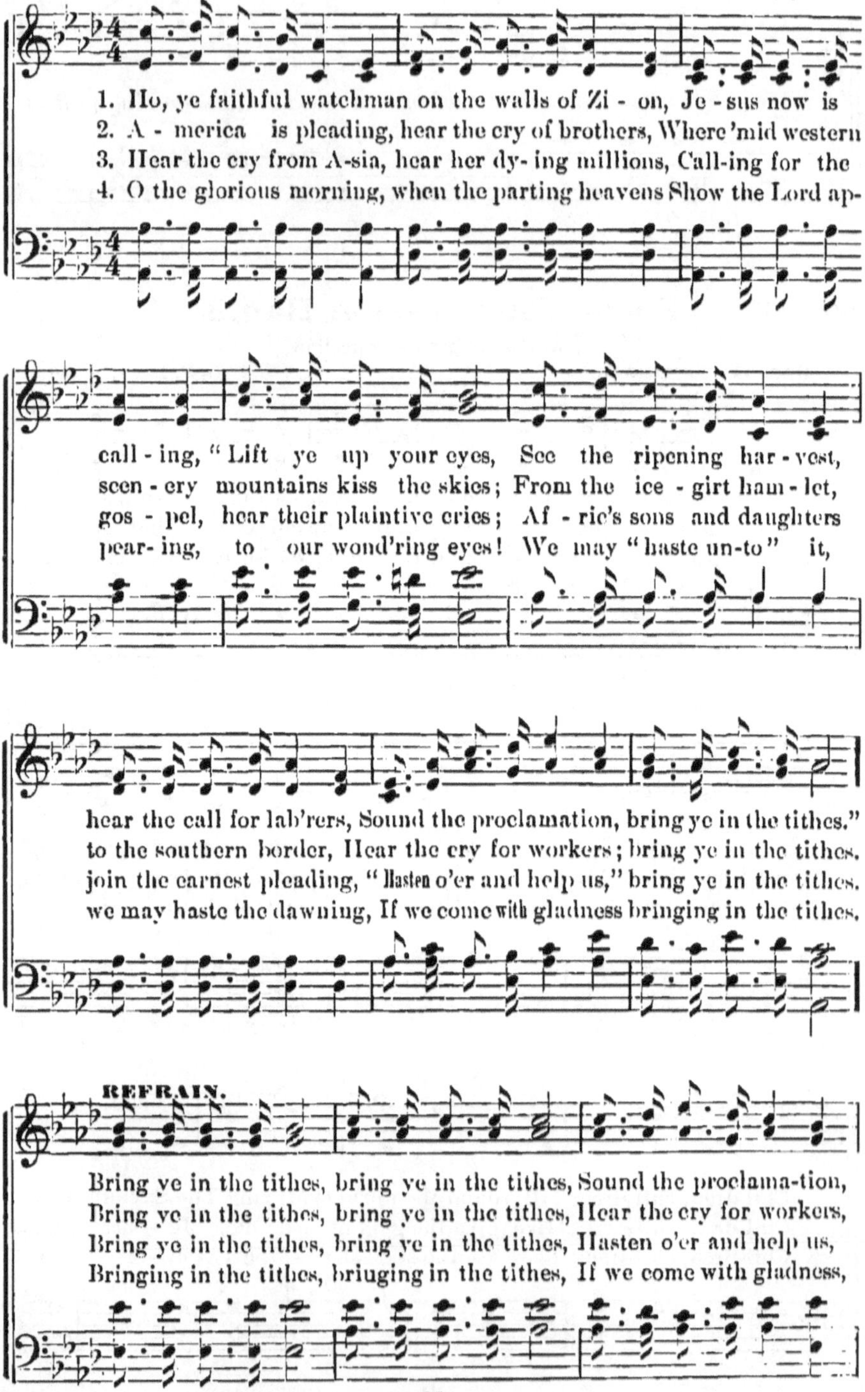

1. Ho, ye faithful watchman on the walls of Zi-on, Je-sus now is call-ing, "Lift ye up your eyes, See the ripening har-vest, hear the call for lab'rers, Sound the proclamation, bring ye in the tithes."
2. A-merica is pleading, hear the cry of brothers, Where 'mid western scen-ery mountains kiss the skies; From the ice-girt ham-let, to the southern border, Hear the cry for workers; bring ye in the tithes.
3. Hear the cry from A-sia, hear her dy-ing millions, Call-ing for the gos-pel, hear their plaintive cries; Af-ric's sons and daughters join the earnest pleading, "Hasten o'er and help us," bring ye in the tithes.
4. O the glorious morning, when the parting heavens Show the Lord ap-pear-ing, to our wond'ring eyes! We may "haste un-to" it, we may haste the dawning, If we come with gladness bringing in the tithes.

REFRAIN.

Bring ye in the tithes, bring ye in the tithes, Sound the proclama-tion,
Bring ye in the tithes, bring ye in the tithes, Hear the cry for workers,
Bring ye in the tithes, bring ye in the tithes, Hasten o'er and help us,
Bringing in the tithes, bringing in the tithes, If we come with gladness,

Bring Ye in the Tithes. Concluded.

bring ye in the tithes; See the ripening har-vest, hear the call for la-b'rers, Sound the proc-la-ma-tion, bring ye in the tithes.
bring ye in the tithes; From the ice-girt ham-let to the southern bor-der, Hear the cry for work-ers, bring ye in the tithes.
bring ye in the tithes; Afric's sons and daughters join the earn-est pleading, Hast-en o'er and help us, bring ye in the tithes.
bringing in the tithes; We may "haste unto" it, we may haste the dawning, If we come with glad-ness, bring-ing in the tithes.

No. 92. Windham.

DANIEL READ.

1. Tho' now the na-tions sit beneath The darkness of o'erspreading death; God will a-rise with light di-vine, On Zi-on's ho-ly towers to shine.
2. That light shall shine on distant lands, And wand'ring tribes, in joyful bands, Shall come, thy glory, Lord to see, And in thy courts to worship thee.
3. O light of Zi-on, now a-rise! Let the glad morning bless our eyes; Ye nations, catch the kindling ray, And hail the splendors of the day.

No. 93. Tell It Out.

"Go ye therefore and teach all nations."—MATT. 28: 19.

F. R. HAVERGAL. H. N. LINCOLN.

1. Tell it out a-mong the na-tions that the Lord is King, Tell it out! tell it out! Tell it out a-mong the na-tions, bid them shout and sing, Tell it out! tell it out! Tell it out with ad-o-ra-tion that he will in-crease, That the

2. Tell it out a-mong the peo-ple that the Savior reigns, Tell it out! tell it out! Tell it out a-mong the heathen, bid them break their chains, Tell it out! tell it out! Tell it out a-mong the weep-ing ones that Je-sus lives, Tell it

3. Tell it out a-mong the peo-ple, Je-sus reigns a-bove, Tell it out! tell it out! Tell it out a-mong the na-tions, that his reign is love, Tell it out! tell it out! Tell it out a-mong the high-ways and the lanes at home, Let it

Tell It Out. Concluded.

mighty King of glo-ry is the King of peace, Tell it out with jubi-
out a-mong the weary ones what rest he gives, Tell it out among the
ring across the mountains and the ocean's foam, That the weary, heavy

la-tion, let the song ne'er cease, Tell it out! tell it out!
sinners that he came to save, Tell it out! tell it out!
la-den, need no long-er roam, Tell it out! tell it out!

Tell it out! tell it out!

No. 94.   Sicilian Hymn.
THOS. KELLEY.   Italian.

1. Yes, we trust the day is breaking; Joy-ful times are near at hand;

{ God, the mighty God, is speaking By his word in ev-'ry land: }
{ When he chooses, When he chooses, Darkness flies at his com-mand. }

2 Let us hail the joyful season,
   Let us hail the dawning ray;
When the Lord appears, there's reason
   To expect a glorious day:
At his presence At his presence
   Gloom and darkness flee away.

3 God of Jacob, high and glorious,
   Let thy people see thy hand;
Let the gospel be victorious
   Through the world, in every land;
And the idols And the idols
   Perish, Lord, at thy command!

No. 95. Beautiful Story.

I. H. B.
ISAAC H. BULLER.

1. Oh, beauti-ful sto-ry, Go, tell it, go, tell it, a-near and a-far,
2. Oh, wonderful Je-sus—Go, tell it, go, tell it to all the world round;
3. Go tell the poor heathen Of Je-sus and pardon—oh, hear the glad strain;

Of Je-sus in glo-ry— Go tell of this lovely, this bright morning star'
From darkness he leads us, Oh, shout the glad tidings, re-ech-o the sound.
A mansion in heaven Awaits all who serve him, with him they shall reign.

CHORUS.

Go, tell . . . to all na - - - tions this beau - - -
Go, tell to all nations this beau-ti-ful sto-ry, Go, tell to all

- - ti-ful sto - - ry, That Christ . . . hath re-
nations this beau-ti-ful sto-ry, That Christ hath redeemed us from

Beautiful Story. Concluded.

No. 96. Zerah.
JOHN H. MORRISON, 1770.

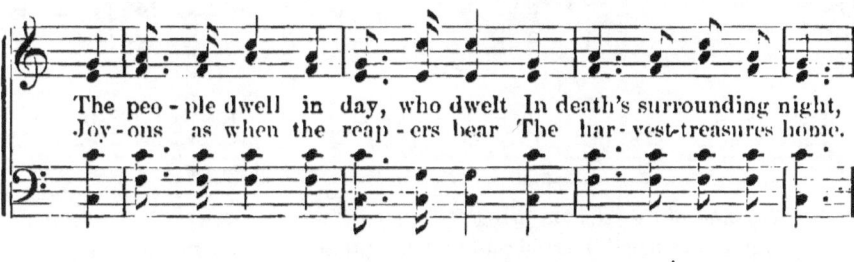

1. The race that long in dark-ness pined Have seen a glorious Light;
2. To hail thy rise, thy bet-ter Sun, The gathering na-tions come,

The peo-ple dwell in day, who dwelt In death's surrounding night,
Joy-ous as when the reap-ers bear The har-vest-treasures home.

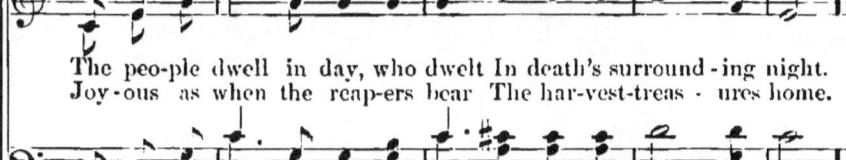

The peo-ple dwell in day, who dwelt In death's surround-ing night.
Joy-ous as when the reap-ers bear The har-vest-treas-ures home.

3 For thou our burden hast removed,
   And quelled th' oppressor's sway,
  Quick as the slaughtered squadrons fell
   In Midian's evil day.

4 To us a Child of hope is born,
   To us a Son is given;
  Him shall the tribes of earth obey,
  Him all the hosts of heaven.

5 His name shall be the Prince of peace,
   For evermore adored;
  The Wonderful, the Counselor,
   The great and mighty Lord.

6 His power increasing, still shall spread;
   His reign no end shall know;
  Justice shall guard his throne above,
   And peace abound below.

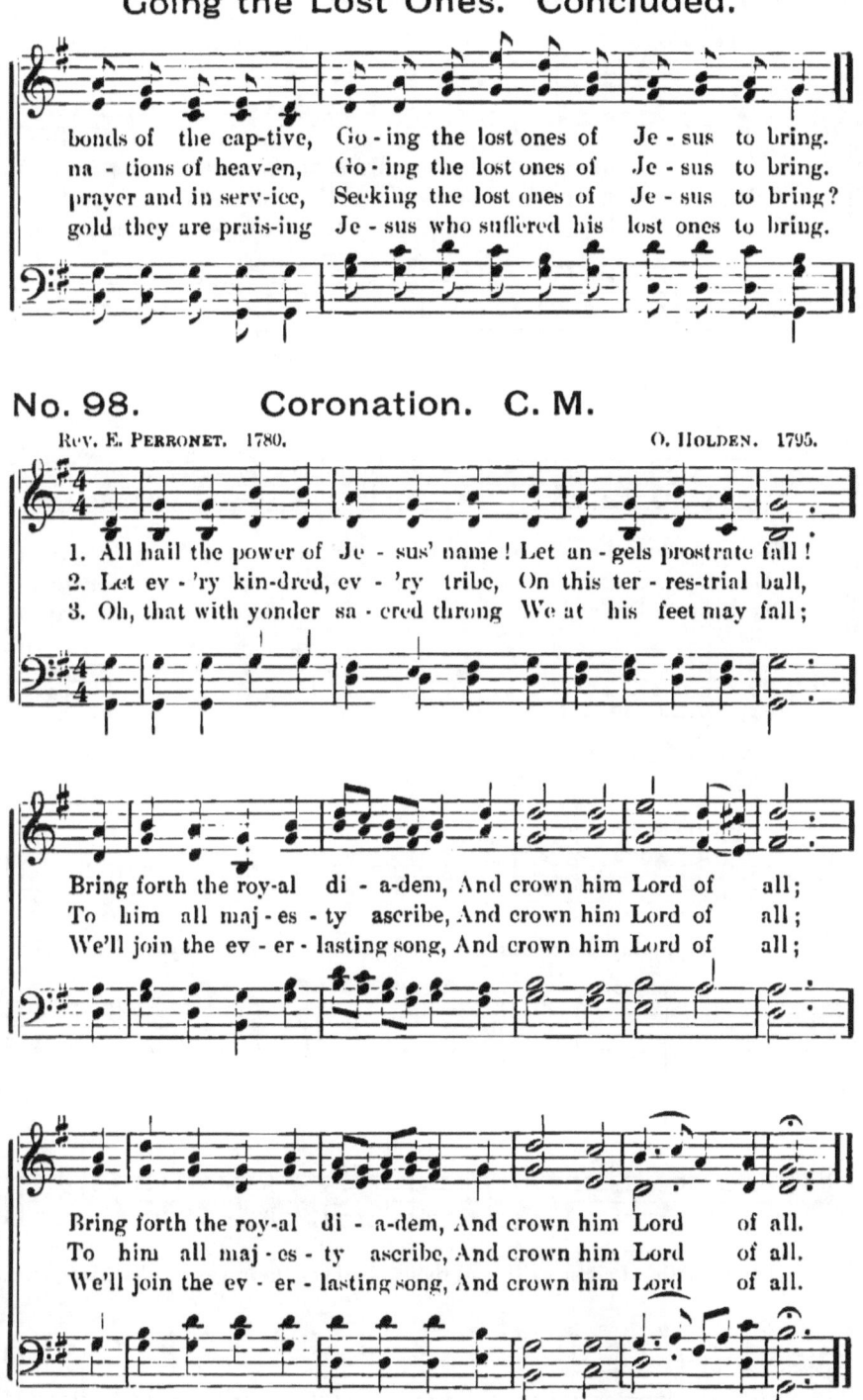

Voice in the Wilderness. Concluded.

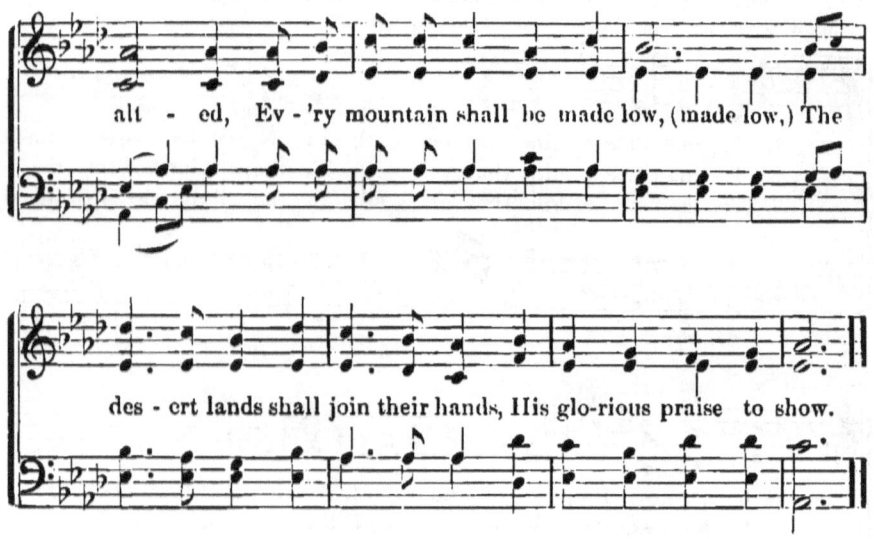

alt - ed, Ev-'ry mountain shall be made low, (made low,) The
des - ert lands shall join their hands, His glo-rious praise to show.

No. 101. Dying for the Knowledge of Jesus.

"*And this is life eternal, that they may know thee . . . and Jesus Christ, whom thou hast sent.*"—JOHN 17: 3.

S. M. BROWN. S. M. BROWN, by per.

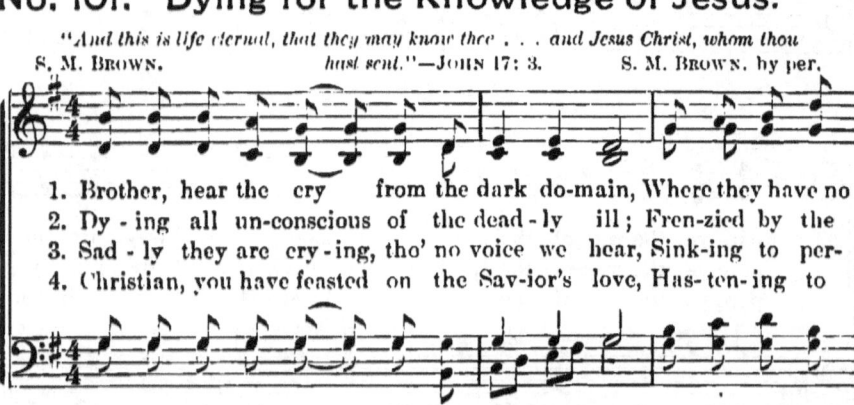

1. Brother, hear the cry from the dark do-main, Where they have no
2. Dy - ing all un-conscious of the dead - ly ill; Fren-zied by the
3. Sad - ly they are cry-ing, tho' no voice we hear, Sink-ing to per-
4. Christian, you have feasted on the Sav-ior's love, Has-ten-ing to

knowledge of the Sav - ior's name; See the dark'ning night, hear the
fe - ver of the fa - tal chill; Blinded by de-cep-tion of the
di - tion, yet they feel no fear; Si - lently they're pleading by their
the joys of the world a - bove; Will you with indiff'rence hear your

Dying for the Knowledge. Concluded.

plain-tive cry, "Send us now the gos-pel or our souls must die."
world's dread foe, Standing on the mar-gin of e - ter - nal woe.
sin and shame, Cry - ing for the knowledge of the Sav - ior's name.
broth-er's cry, "Send us now the gos-pel or our souls must die?"

CHORUS.

Broth-er, they are cry-ing, cry-ing un - to you, "Save us from e-
ter - nal shame;" Trembling on the brink of the world of woe,
Dy - ing for the know-ledge of the Sav - ior's name.

Gather them into the Fold. Concluded.

O-pen to all is the gos-pel door, Gather them into the fold.
Lead them along to the home above, Gather them into the fold.

CHORUS.

Gath — — er them in, . . . gath — — —
Gath-er them, gath-er them in - to the fold, Gath-er them,

— — er them in, . . . Gath — — er them
gath-er them in - to the fold, Gath - er them care - ful - ly,

in, , . . . Gath - er them in - to the fold.
gath-er them prayerfully,

Arm of the Lord. Concluded.

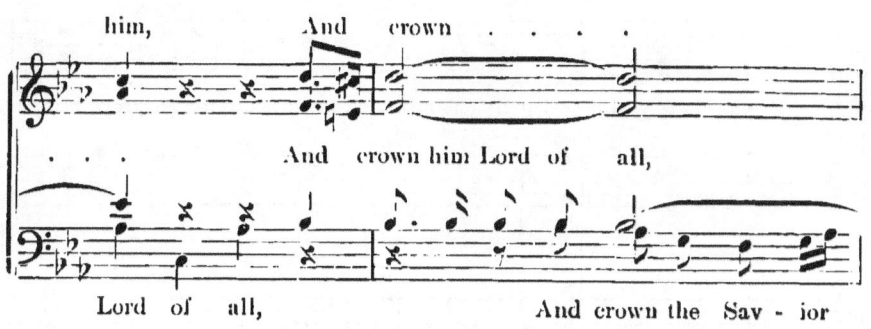

No. 104. He is the Lord, Our God.

J. M. Hunt.

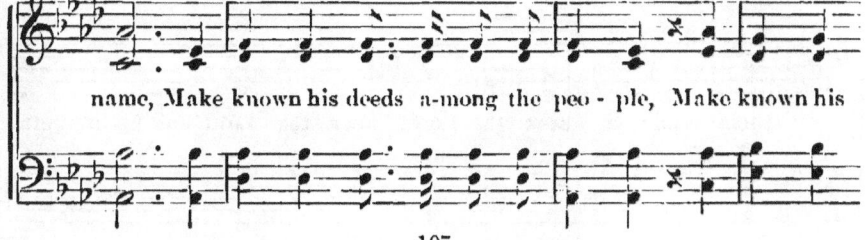

He is the Lord, Our God. Continued.

108

He is the Lord, Our God. Concluded.

Jesus, I my Cross have Taken. Concluded.

ev - 'ry fond am - bi - tion, All I've sought, or hoped, or known, Yet how
thou shalt smile upon me, God of wis - dom, love and might, Foes may
not in grief to harm me, While thy love is left to me, O, 't were

rich is my con - di - tion! God and heaven are still my own!
hate, and friends may shun me, Show thy face, and all is bright.
not in joy to charm me, Were that joy unmixed with thee.

No. 106.   Crown Him Lord of All.

PERRONET.   J. M. HUNT.

1. All hail the power of Jesus' name! Let an - gels prostrate fall!
2. Let ev - 'ry kin-dred, ev - 'ry tribe, On this ter - res-trial ball,
3. Oh, that with yon-der sa-cred throng We at his feet may fall;

Crown Him Lord of All. Concluded.

No. 107. **If I Were a Voice.**

J. M. HUNT, by per.

1. If I were a voice, a persuasive voice, That could travel the wide world through, I would fly on the beams of the morning light, And speak to men with a gentle might, And tell them to be
2. If I were a voice, a consoling voice, I'd fly on the wings of the air; The homes of sorrow and guilt I'd seek, And calm and truthful words I'd speak, To save them from de-
3. If I were a voice, a convincing voice, I'd travel with the wind, And wherever I saw the nations torn, By war-fare, jealousy, spite or scorn, Or hatred of their
4. If I were a voice, an immortal voice, I would fly the earth around, And wherever man to his idols bowed, I'd publish in notes both long and loud The Gospel's joyful

If I Were a Voice. Concluded.

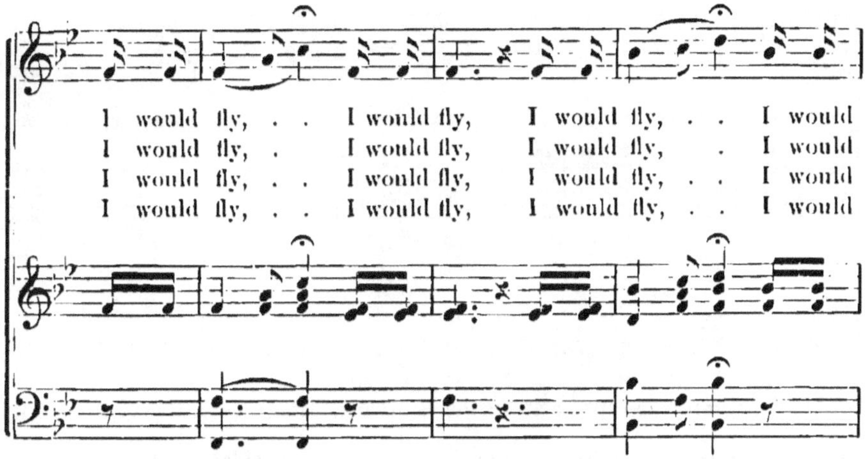

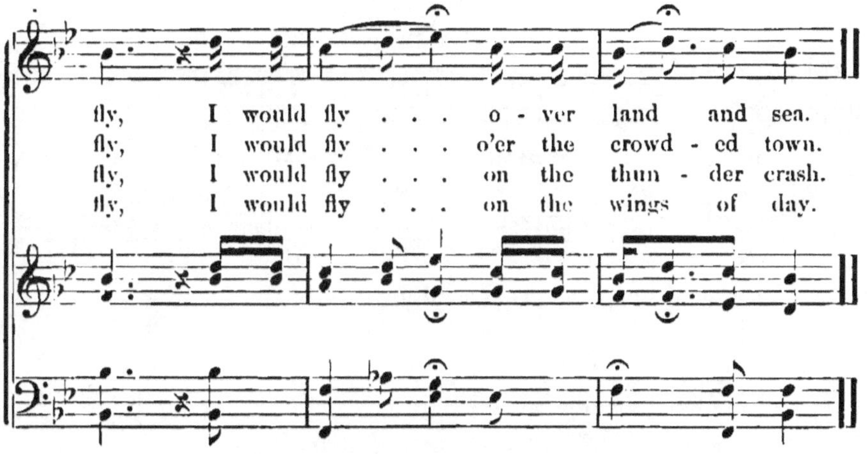

I would fly, . . I would fly, I would fly, . . I would
I would fly, . I would fly, I would fly, . I would
I would fly, . . I would fly, I would fly, . . I would
I would fly, . . I would fly, I would fly, . . I would

fly, I would fly . . . o - ver land and sea.
fly, I would fly . . . o'er the crowd - ed town.
fly, I would fly . . . on the thun - der crash.
fly, I would fly . . . on the wings of day.

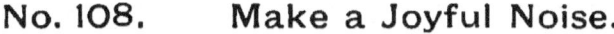

No. 108. Make a Joyful Noise.

G. F. Root, by per.

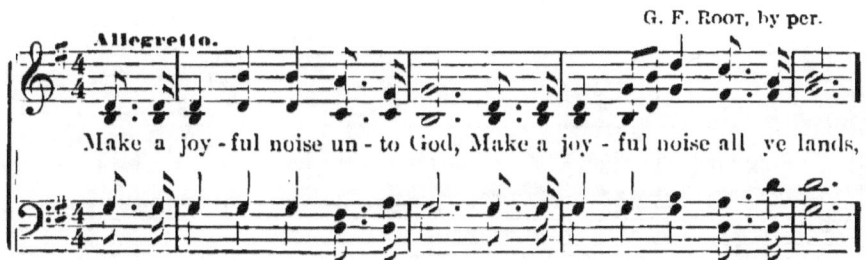

Allegretto.
Make a joy - ful noise un - to God, Make a joy - ful noise all ye lands,

No. 109.   Praise God from Whom.

J. M. HUNT.

Praise God from whom all bless-ings flow, Praise him all crea-tures here be-low; Praise God from whom all bless-ings flow, Praise God all crea-tures here be-low; Praise him a-bove, ... Praise him a-bove, ... Praise him a-bove, ye heavenly host, ye heavenly host, Praise him a-bove, ... Praise him a-bove, ye heavenly host; Praise him a-

Praise God from Whom. Concluded.

INDEX.

TITLES IN SMALL CAPS—FIRST LINES IN ROMAN.

Home Mission Songs, from No. 1 to No. 57.
Foreign Mission Songs, from No. 58 to No. 101.
Miscellaneous Songs, from No. 102 to end.

	NUMBER
All Hail the Power of Jesus' Name	98, 106
AMERICA	41
America I love all other lands above	57
ANTIOCH	85
ARMY OF THE LORD	53
ARISE, MY SOUL, ARISE	76
ARM OF THE LORD	103
Arm of the Lord, Awake	103
Awake, Awake, put on thy Strength	1
Away, away o'er the Ocean Wave	72
AWAY TO-DAY	99
BEAUTIFUL STORY	95
BLOW YE THE TRUMPET, BLOW	75
BRING THEM IN	26
BRING YE IN THE TITHES	91
Brother hear the Cry from the	101
CHURCH OF GOD, AWAKE	45
Church of God whose conquering	45
CHRIST FOR THE WORLD	67
Christ for the World we Sing	67
CLING TO THE BIBLE	11
Cling to the Bible Though all else	11
COMETH A BLESSING DOWN	15
COME JOIN THE ARMY	4
COME, COME AND SEE	63
CORONATION	98
CROWN HIM	89
Crown Him, Crown Him every Nation	89
CROWN HIM LORD OF ALL	106
DEAR NATIVE LAND	57
DEAR CHILDREN FAR AWAY	71
Do not say, O Christian Reaper	35
Down the Column of the Ages	62
DUKE STREET	80
DYING FOR THE KNOWLEDGE OF JESUS	101
EVERY ONE TO THE WORK OF JESUS	70
FORM YOUR MISSION BANDS	90
Form, Form your Mission Bands	90
From all the Dark Places	84
From Greenland's Icy Mountains	71, 82
GATHER THEM INTO THE FOLD	102
GO WORK IN MY VINEYARD	64

	NUMBER
Go to the Hedges and Broad	102
Go ye out to the Fields for the	18
GO FORTH TO THE FIELD	14
GO IN THE STRENGTH OF JESUS	36
Go when the Skies are Brightest	36
GO WIELD THE SICKLE'S BLADE	35
Go Work in my Vineyard To-day	43
GO AND LABOR	79
GOING THE LOST ONES TO BRING	97
Going Away from the Home of Their	97
Great God the Nations of the Earth	60
Great God whose Universal Sway	56
HARWELL	9
Hark! Ten Thousand Harps and	9
Hark! the Voice of Jesus crying	48
Hark! 'tis the Shepherd's Voice I hear	26
Hear the Angels Gladly Singing	13
HEAR THE CRY FROM HEATHEN LANDS	86
Hear the Gospel Invitation	63
HERE AM I SEND ME	48
HEBRON	56
HE IS THE LORD OUR GOD	104
How many Sheep are Straying	33
Ho! Ye Faithful Watchman on the	91
HUNT	74
IF I WERE A VOICE	107
I need not go to India	22
IN THE CROSS	10
In the Cross of Christ I Glory	10
In the Vineyard of the Master	79
In the Vineyard of the Lord	7
In a Distant Land, my Brother	99
In Lands full of Darkness Across	71
Into the Tent where a Gypsy Boy lay	41
JESUS I MY CROSS HAVE TAKEN	105
JESUS SHALL REIGN WHERE'ER THE SUN	58, 73
Joy to the World, the Lord is Come	85
KEEP THE BANNER UNFURLED	54
KEDESH	69
Lift up your Eyes on the Fields	20
Lift up your Eyes, Behold and see	37
LITTLE GLEANERS	34
LITTLE GLEANERS BAND	2

INDEX.

	NUMBER		NUMBER
Look Unto the Fields	18	The Bible, the Bible more Precious	55
Look up, Behold the Fields	21	The Fields are White, 'tis Harvest Time	17
Lost Names	29	The Harvest Time	21
		The Little Missionary	22
Make a Joyful Noise	108	The Harvest is White	37
Missionary Hymn	82	The Missionary Triumph	1
My Country 'tis of Thee	41	The Fields are now White and	27
Not to a Man of Dollars	15	The Lord's Prayer	25
Not yet Beneath our Captain's Feet	61	The Master hath Need of the Reapers	52
Now is the Harvest Time	20		
O Beautiful Story, go tell it	95	The Mighty Song	62
O give Thanks Unto the Lord	104	The Word of Life	72
O, Where are the Reapers	16	The Kingdom Coming	84
O, Where are the Reapers that Garner	16	The Morning Light is Breaking	87
O Lord of Heaven and Earth and	23	The Race that Long in Darkness	96
Old Hundred	39	The Light of the World is Jesus	68
On the Mountain's Top Appearing	46	The Whole World was Lost in the	68
Open the Door for the Children	24	There's a Cry from Macedonia	59
O Soul Look up and Thou	53	There's a Wail from the Islands of	65
Our Country for Jesus	40	They Lived and they were Useful	29
Our Country for Jesus, of this will I sing	40	Thank God for the Bible	51
Our Country for Jesus, the Land of the Free	54	Though now the Nations sit	92
Our Father who art in Heaven	25	There is a Fountain Filled with	12
Over against the Treasury of the	8	'Tis Never too Late to be Sowing the	49
O When Shall These Glad Tidings Spread	60	'Tis the Voice of Him that	100
		Toiling in the Vineyard	3
Peace on Earth	13	Trust on	5
Praise God from Whom	39, 109	Trust on, Trust on Believer	5
Precious Fountain	12	Up, Brother, Up	31
		Up, Friends of Jesus, the Harvest	50
Rally to the Master's Call	7	Up in the Morning and Away to	3
Ready to Harvest	27	Voice in the Wilderness	100
Rejoice and Shout Aloud	61	Wander the Weary o'er the Land	31
Ring the Bells	66	Waiting is the Golden Harvest	28
Ring, Ring the Bells, the Sweet	66	Watchman Tell Me	78
		We are a Little Gleaning Band	34
Salvation, O the Joyful Sound	83	We will Go	30
Seeking the Lost Sheep	33	We will Go in the Strength of	30
See the Fields are White for Harvest	2	We are Coming	42
Shout the Tidings	6	We have Heard Thy Gentle Voice	42
Shout the Tidings of Salvation	6	Webb	87
Shout for Gladness	77	What Shall we Give to God	23
Shout for Gladness Sons of Zion	77	Who will Reply	17
Ship of Zion	65	Who will Go and Work To-day	28
Sicilian Hymn	94	Windham	92
Something to Do	49	Work for your Master	19
Soon may the Last Glad Song	80	Work To-day	43
Speak some Word Where'er Thou	64	Work and Pray	50
Stand Up for Jesus	38, 88		
Stand Up, Stand Up for Jesus	38, 88	Ye Nations of the Earth	81
		Ye Nations Round the Earth Rejoice	81
Take my Life and let it Be	32	Yes we Trust the Day is Breaking	94
Tell it Again	44	Yes my Native Land I love Thee	69
Tell it Out	93		
Tell it Out Among the Nations	93	Zion	46
The Widow's Mite	8	Zion Stands with Hills Surrounded	47
The Bible	55	Zerah	96

www.ingramcontent.com/pod-product-compliance
Lightning Source LLC
Chambersburg PA
CBHW020128170426
43199CB00009B/688